WHEN
SMART PEOPLE
WORK FOR
DUMB BOSSES

WHEN SMART PEOPLE WORK FOR DUMB BOSSES

How to Survive in a Crazy and Dysfunctional Workplace

WILLIAM LUNDIN, PHD
KATHLEEN LUNDIN

McGraw-Hill

New York San Francisco Washington, D.C. Auckland Bogotá
Caracas Lisbon London Madrid Mexico City Milan
Montreal New Delhi San Juan Singapore
Sydney Tokyo Toronto

Library of Congress Cataloging-in-Publication Data applied for

McGraw-Hill

A Division of The McGraw·Hill Companies

1 2 3 4 5 6 7 8 9 0   FGRFGR   9 0 3 2 1 0 9 8

ISBN 0-07-039147-5

The editing supervisor for this book was Patricia V. Amoroso, and the production supervisor was Clare Stanley. It was set in Garamond by Teresa F. Leaden of McGraw-Hill's Professional Book Group composition unit.

Illustrations by Steven Lundin.

This publication is designed to provide accurate and authoritative information in regard to the subject matter covered. It is sold with the understanding that the publisher is not engaged in rendering legal, accounting, or other professional service. If legal advice or other expert assistance is required, the services of a competent professional person should be sought.

    —from a declaration of principles jointly adopted by a committee of the American Bar Association and a Committee of publishers.

 This book is printed on recycled, acid-free paper containing a minimum of 50% recycled, de-inked fiber.

McGraw-Hill books are available at special quantity discounts to use as premiums and sales promotions, or for use in corporate training programs. For more information, please write to the Director of Special Sales, McGraw-Hill, 11 West 19th Street, New York, NY 10011. Or contact your local bookstore.

To the Office Depot check-out person who, when she saw the title of this book, spontaneously caught its meaning. She said, "You know, employees learn from their mistakes, bosses don't."

CONTENTS

PREFACE

Awaken people's curiosity. It is enough to open minds; do not overload them.

ANATOLE FRANCE

We have got to have the ugly facts in order to protect us from the official view of reality.

BILL MOYERS

Welcome to your world of work, with all its blunders, irrationalities, superstitions, mistakes, errors, follies, fads, and gross injustices—what we call dumbness. This book is but a small part of a tapestry of dumb behavior from antiquity to the present. Dumbness is a field that attracts authors who need to expose irrationality and hypocrisy. We are in this category. In today's work-hard, don't complain, take care of yourself, feel-good society, this is politically *incorrect* material.

Humans come by dumbness (the inexplicably profound error) honestly. A survey funded by the National Endowment for the Humanities demonstrated that it is possible to graduate from 78 percent of the nation's colleges and universities without ever taking a course in the history of Western civilization. The following are examples of what isn't being learned.

The Mississippi Scheme in the early eighteenth century almost ruined France with a mad frenzy of speculation for land in Louisiana. Its perpetrator, John Law, wrote, "I confess that I have committed many faults. I committed them because I am a man, and all men are liable to error." The mania then for easy profit overtook people in every station of life, from the humblest beggar to the richest merchant, all of whom found themselves richer by the thousands within the space of 1 day. John Law died destitute.

Bernard Baruch, leading financier and statesman, commented on the Great Depression, "I have always thought that if, in the lamentable era of the 'New Economics,' culminating in 1929, even in the very presence of dizzily spiraling prices, we had all continuously repeated, 'two and two still makes four,' much of the evil might have been averted."

Fearing the misinterpretation of a recent, tragic blunder, Vietnam vet George Swiers wrote, "If we do not speak of it, others will surely rewrite the script. Each of the body bags, all of the mass graves will be reopened and their contents abracadabraed into a noble cause."

New York Times columnist Russell Baker said, "I don't suppose anyone can make it through a whole lifetime here in the twentieth century twilight zone without an occasional suspicion that he is living in a global booby hatch."

Dumb behavior has ever been with us, hand-in-hand with brilliantly conceived achievements. Thomas Jefferson, whose keen intellect pilloried would-be autocrats, said that once a man strives for power, "rottenness begins in his conduct." It's gotten worse today because more is at stake.

"To err is human" implies a naiveté, and innocence, being dumb but not malicious. But to err in the face of contradictory evidence, the usual kind of business dumbness, is a form of evil. The workplace is composed of the innocent error and the willfully stupid deed.

In 1841, many irrational acts were gathered together in a book, *Memoirs of Extraordinary Popular Delusions*. It was brought up to date in 1932 by Charles Mackay as *Extraordinary Popular Delusions* and *The Madness of Crowds* (15). Its topics include schemes to defraud the gullible, tulipomania, alchemy, witch mania, fortunetelling, the misadventures of the Crusades, and many other idiocies. Military mistakes and blunders are a favorite topic. *Lying Truths* (4) takes apart conventional thought about work, education, psychiatry, statistics, and religion. *The Blunder Book* (6) recounts colossal errors, slip-ups, and mistakes that have changed the course of history. *The March of Folly* (26) is devoted to the dumbness of governments, from the Trojan Horse to the United States in Vietnam.

Dumbness has affected everything from the midseventeenth-century craze for tulips, to King George's loss of the American colonies, Custer's Last Stand, the Charge of the Light Brigade, the sinking of the *Titanic*, the loss of the automotive market to Japanese car manufacturers, the rejection of the xerographic process by Kodak, to the Valujet crash.

Even before humans were classified as *Homo sapiens*, wise man, in preference to something closer to the truth, *Homo sapiens/stupidus*, wise/dumb man, we've glossed over our weaknesses and dark sides. We see the dumb acts we perform as aberrations rather than as parts of our core personalities.

Weird, irrational solutions to cope with the uncertainties of life arise in every era. If a plague occurs, burn a witch. Defy established dogma, burn the heretic. Crops fail, offer a human sacrifice. Too much rain, pound on drums. Not enough rain, pound on drums. Assure good luck, carry a rabbit's foot. Versions of human sacrifice and drum pounding still exist. Appease the god Wall Street, downsize the workforce. Fire up employees, send them to seminars. Boost quality, make speeches and hang 150 banners. Placate investors, axe the president.

ACKNOWLEDGENTS

We owe a special debt of thanks to all the people we interviewed; their stories wrote this book. All we did was extrapolate meaning and derive lessons for the reader. But before this current group of stories took its present form, there were many other incidents that pointed toward the dumb boss syndrome. So to the thousands of employees and managers with whom we've worked, and who were willing to confide in us, we owe a huge and unending debt. Regarding the evolution of the book itself: it would not have been possible without the enthusiastic support of our sponsoring editor, Mary Glenn. It was Mary who immediately clicked-in to the concept, and pushed the project along. Special thanks to Pattie Amoroso and her staff of copy editors. We received editorial help from Mark Frazel, Carey Lundin, and Steven Lundin, and we thank them. Finally, as married co-authors who are still talking to one another, and planning other projects, we want to record our mutual thanks.

INTRODUCTION

It must be borne in mind that my design is not to write histories, but lives. And the most glorious exploits do not always furnish us with the clearest discoveries of virtue or vice in men . . . so I must be allowed to give my more particular attention to the marks and indications of the souls of men . . .

PLUTARCH

The true stories of people in the workplace are seldom printed. There are such familiar sounds ("I'm all stressed out while my manager plays computer games in his office."), familiar smells ("There's not a breath of fresh air in this damned building."), and familiar gripes ("We used to sit around and wonder: How did those people get up there?"). In the course of our work we've interviewed, taught, and observed the behavior of hundreds of men and women at all corporate levels, representing many diverse industries. The 45 interviews for this book were recently obtained. However, the information in them is no different from what we've always known. The stories represent so universal a theme that to get 45, 75, or 100 incidents all you have to do is sit down and talk with 45, 75, or 100 people. We have found no exceptions. Their stories are your stories.

WHO, WHAT, WHERE

Ordinary people, not celebrities, were interviewed. We promised anonymity. We did not change the essence of their words. They coped with impossible to believe bosses and remained sane (at a cost) in blindly run organizations. Meet managers, supervisors, hourly workers, educators, healthcare professionals, engineers, trainers, team leaders, editors, and former CEOs. Information was obtained in widespread locations, and we tape-recorded in diners, restaurants, bookstores, on convention floors, around kitchen tables, on patios, in their offices, and in ours.

Low morale, inadequately motivated performance, compromise, and lack of appreciation mark dumb organizations. Insensitivity and deprecation of effort mark the dumb boss. The reward for that treatment defines today's American workplace, a pressure job for anyone who wants one and an uncertain career ladder for a minority of others.

Our findings are not reassuring as a measure of morale and loyalty nor as a predictor of what lies ahead. Each storyteller grasps for meaning. The undercurrents of all interviews—you hear it in their words—are bewilderment and bafflement.

DUMBNESS IS NOT A POPULAR THEME

We've searched for "dumbness" as a generic concept and couldn't find many references. Some are in the Preface; others are in the References. Information about human fallibility makes people uncomfortable. For example: "Less obvious is the damage it did to intellect, discrimination, honesty, individuality, complexity, ambiguity, and irony, not to mention privacy and wit." A statement about an atrociously run company? It could be, but no. It's from *Wartime*, an important book documenting the mistakes, absurdities, miscalculations, and flawed leadership in World War II (5).

War and business resonate together. To succeed in either requires flawless strategic planning and execution, precision in the movement of supplies and people, technological innovation, clever propaganda, and enormous infusions of money. There are parallels in structure also: in hierarchy, the unquestioned role of authority, and the necessity for teamwork. In both, when stupidity takes over, it is the common soldiers and their officers, employees and their supervisors, who get the dirty end of the stick. Dumbness goes downhill.

Documenting Behavior

Dumb behavior is motivated by self-love and ego, which block the capacity for empathy. It plays to Wall Street's definition of success, encouraging momentary profitability over long-range planning and creating panic behavior in management. Chasing the latest management fad, restructuring, and downsizing are symptoms.

A long-lingering perception is that bosses are not trusted and make serious errors with terrible consequences. That knowledge powered the early trade union movement. Blue-collar workers are now being joined in spirit, if not yet action, by some of their former managers who have been downsized into similar grass-roots wisdom. From business, to education, to healthcare, to politics, surveys report that people on the top are judged to be dumb.

Commonly Understood but Seldom Mentioned

Incidents of dumbness have no agreed-upon name. Gravity and relativity, too, at one time had no name, even though those physical forces entered into all transactions in the universe. Dumbness is assumed to be normal and is seldom spoken about. Also, and this is most significant, dumbness does not become the focus of research. Geoffry Regan (21) refers to it as "blunders." Barbara Tuchman calls it "folly and perversity." Her "folly" criteria are particularly applicable to the workplace—it must be counterproductive; an alternative course of action should exist; the policy in question should be that of a group. She says, "Folly's appearance is independent of era or locality; it is timeless and universal . . . It is unrelated to type of regime . . . folly or perversity is inherent in individuals." (26) We reach identical conclusions in our study of business folly.

What's the Point of This Book?

The number of feel-good, here-comes-the-parade, spiritually tinged publications have overwhelmed all other depictions of

the workplace. Except for the Dilbert series, these publications demean people's inherent urge for independent, solu-
tion-seeking, and self-fulfilling action. The average employee
is made to feel lucky to be where he or she is. In other
words, don't ask why things are the way they are at work and
don't tell others how you really feel. This book is a more
evenhanded depiction of work.

We bring balance to the field. Not to be a spoilsport, but
we regard the "seven-step," "hundred best ways" approach
to understanding life and work as interesting fiction. Read
them if you need them. They are pie in the sky at best and
misleading at worst. Work is different from what the seven
and one hundred-type books would have you believe. And
it's 180° different from the images painted by academics,
celebrity coaches, and self-glorifying CEOs. Who sees most
clearly? It doesn't matter. Our own vision propels us more
than others.

Will you be able to transform your dysfunctional organization? It would take more guts than people are currently
exhibiting. Job loss is a fear in spite of a strong economy. So
what might you learn? That work is more isolating in spite of
the emphasis on teams is one lesson. That compromise is an
adaptive technique is another lesson. That as corporate power
strengthens, yours weakens. And that knowing these things
and listening to your peers might stir a sense of survival
defined more in your terms than your boss's.

We need to know more about how dumbness affects the
millions who do their jobs daily, uncomplaining, remaining
silent, and taken for granted. Employees who don't aspire to
leadership should not be victimized. They should be encouraged to contribute without fear of running into the workplace bully.

HOW THE BOOK IS ORGANIZED

The book is an integration of oral history and analysis. The
interviews are minimally edited. Each story is followed by an
interpretive section, "Meanings and Lessons." "Meanings" is

the jumping-off point. In that section, we direct your attention to a few key elements. We also talk about broader issues of work. "Lessons" is just that: focused summations and metaphors that offer insights into survival.

Part One, "The Heart of Dumbness," is the central core. It is about the genesis of dumbness and its perpetuation. The three chapters describe dumb leaders, dumb organizations, and the dumbing-down of corporate cultures. Stories include managed care, hospitals, banking, brokerage and real estate, oil, education, publishing, TV, manufacturing, mail order, and municipal services.

Part Two, "Faces of Dumbness," shows the consequences of dumbness upon efforts to increase productivity and market share. The three chapters focus on teams, quality, and empowerment. The industries covered include biomedical, electronics, automotive, healthcare, education, manufacturing, training, and food services.

What's Smart and What's Dumb?

Anyone at work can be smart one minute and dumb the next. Because our emphasis falls on the dumb side doesn't mean that the fools, ogres, idiots, monsters, and blindsided bosses are dumb all the time or that their IQs are low. At some time, during the same day, many of us are employees as well as bosses, heroes as well as villains. We're here, there, all over the place, pulled and pushed, and living many different roles. There's nothing intrinsically unhealthy about playing many roles because they actually replicate life itself: infant, child, sibling, adolescent, schoolmate, buddy, adult, team player, parent, grandparent. But in the workplace, it's happening much too fast. There is not enough time to learn multiple roles.

We live in an organizational hall of mirrors. You'll see yourself as leader, powerful in one reflection, and follower, weak in another. Your reflected image—magnified, diminished, and distorted—is like elements of a Freudian dream. Such forced and rapid redefinitions of identity create errors in judgment, planning, decision making, and relationships with others. Management has gotten smarter about how to run lean, profitable organizations but dumber about the needs of employees who live inside them.

People sense that the number of negative consequences created by dumbness follows a gradient of power: The more power an organization has, the more pain and confusion it can inflict on others. People also know that smartness, too, follows a gradient: The closer you are to a big, dumb mistake made by a big, dumb leader, the smarter you need to be to confine and neutralize it. Many know about worst-case scenarios of dumb cultures which account for the actual or near downfalls of well-known companies. Those unfortunate events prompt people to ask, "How can so many smart people make so many dumb mistakes?" The comment is much too kind. In those situations, leaders were truly dumb, cloning dumbness around them.

It hurts when the smart thing you feel you've done is judged dumb by your boss. For example, in your role as supervisor, you express concern to your employee about an illness in her family. Your manager tells you it is a mistake to get too personal with your workers.

You're a CEO and contract for a new quality program. Your production managers know the program can't work like all the others haven't worked because morale is terrible. You refuse to believe it. You once were named the small businessperson of the year, so you feel you're smart. Your managers think you're dumb but don't dare tell you. You were not on this year's "best" list and your name has already been forgotten. You've had your run.

Look Inside the System

Social analysts stand back and organize weighty global economic data in order to explain the present and predict the future. If the world's economy were like the body of a dragon, our nation would occupy the major parts of the digestive system—if the analogy isn't offensive—where raw materials are digested and power the rest of the organism. A constantly active, never-tiring process, we churn out new technologies, ideas, and products by the ton. Of course, some of it is waste. But most of it is what the rest of the world wants to emulate and buy—and they do.

Yet how many experts in business clothes want to go into the bowels of a dragon? A few, but not many. Until more do, all the public will get is the black box of big issue analysis. The question "but how does it happen?" is seldom answered. That's what we'll be looking at in this book—where the smart and dumb, good and bad gurgling goes on.

Every little guy thinks he can do it better than the boss. That's part of a national myth about the cocky, self-educated, pragmatic, independent citizen, which no longer makes sense. Today, that little guy includes middle managers as well.

Anyone observing leadership stupidity feels smarter than the boss. Is there truth in those feelings? Do the men and women underneath see and understand more than the people above them? Or are employees merely singing (and dreaming) another version of an old song about equality?

A DANGEROUS GAME

We are all contributors. We all move society along on a precarious equilibrium that's not too dumb and not too smart. When the equilibrium shifts toward smart, we live for a time in a golden age. When it's unbalanced toward dumb, there are catastrophes such as the two world wars, the Great Depression, the botched response to the containment of AIDS and Vietnam.

An equilibrium between smart and dumb is not desirable because blunders, follies, and perversities are always lurking. In a globalized world, the dumb reaction, which once might have been contained, can turn into a huge disaster (Asia's financial meltdown is an example). It's almost impossible to neutralize previously localized episodes of dumbness.

WE'RE STILL COMPROMISING

Here's what people readily talk about when an organization is top-heavy with dumb bosses. The supervisor you expected to be fired turns up managing your department, people don't laugh, people don't talk, tools and reports disappear, trust is destroyed, loyalty exists only in late-night war movies, and people you've known for years lose their jobs.

When bosses get the reputation of being dumb too often, a long time can elapse before anything disastrous happens to their careers. In fact, as employees are quick to point out, for high-profile leaders, it's often the opposite. They get promoted. But when employees are regarded as dumb, they are often quickly disposed of.

The seeds of a backlash exist against all authority, where now blue- and white-collar employees equally target the higher-ups as the source of their frustration. It is no surprise, therefore, that the American Enterprise Institute/Roper Center reported (*Wall Street Journal*, December 23, 1997) the degree of trust in the federal government hit a 40-year low to 20 percent in 1997 from a 1958 high of 80 percent. Even though each person can experience only his or her personal disillusion, all share a hurtful memory—the panic and guilt suffered as a result of downsizing. Those feelings have been partly attenuated, although layoffs continue. Fear may be below the threshold of awareness (but barely), while organizational voraciousness at the expense of people continues its maddening game of bigger is better.

People do not trust what they see and are told by their government or by their employers. Self worth on the job, as you will read, is being trifled with. Futures are being foreshortened. Predictability has been replaced by a desperate acceptance of chaos. Is there, then, any place where employees can find stability? There is. We are convinced, having worked with hundreds of people, that in spite of every negative influence exerted upon them by unfeeling bosses, employees still want to be worthy of their work.

LESSON

The immaturity of your leader does not define who you are. The definition of your worth as an employee lies in your own history.

THE HEART
OF DUMBNESS

TRULY DUMB BOSSES

*There are two races of men in this world, but only these two —the
"race" of the decent man and the "race" of the indecent man. Both are
found everywhere; they penetrate into all groups of society.*

VIKTOR E. FRANKL

Dumb bosses create havoc. They believe themselves superi-
or to others and refuse to consider ideas that contradict
their own. It's a leadership craziness born of nobody knows
exactly what. Dumb bosses terrorize and tease, shredding
employees' feelings like irrelevant memos. They make people
sick. They are feared, envied, and loathed. How can an organization tolerate managers who seem to suspend rules of emotional hygiene and sicken the minds and bodies of their
employees? How can distressed employees produce a quality
product?

One answer is corporate, rather than employee, survival.
Another answer is paradoxical: Employees identify with and
defend their companies no matter how dysfunctional. The
process is not completely conscious, and there are numerous
examples in this book. The first two interviews in this chapter
are the anchor stories. Together, they epitomize what we
mean by the truly dumb boss.

A dysfunction-inducing boss plays a powerful mentoring
role in the lives of employees. Often bound together for years,
the dumb boss and victimized employees develop strange
interpersonal accommodations. Irrationality builds and ampli-
fies itself as in a closed space until the dumb boss's words
start to make sense. Smart employees who should know better
accept the dumbest duties. Such victim behavior is not unusual in hostage-taking situations. When we see it reported at
work, even though on a reduced scale, we know more pathol-
ogy exists than society is willing to talk about.

3

Divisions and departments exist within large organizations that revolve around a leader's bizarre behavior. There are smaller enterprises where a dumb leader's style will seldom be influenced by more enlightened ideas of management. Sit among these people with power, as we do, and you hear good words and see good books, but mostly it's fluff.

How many dumb bosses are there? One in five, in ten, in fifty? Approach a dozen friends and more than half will verify the existence of a dumb boss in their lives. Extrapolate that number: There are more dumb bosses than people who live beneath the poverty line, more than all the baby boomers, more than the populations of our largest cities taken together. In epidemiological terms, we're talking about a pandemic event, bigger than a plague and bigger than an epidemic.

Truly dumb bosses are the misguided knights of poor organizational leadership. These bosses are convinced they are reading human nature correctly and that employees are lazy, untrustworthy, and have no worthwhile ideas. When leaders to whom they report absolve them on the basis of bottom-line criteria—we're making money so how bad can things really be?—you know it's a losing battle.

Whatever creates the truly dumb boss—genes, a toxic emotional environment, crises of change, or cellular memories of a fight for survival which began millions of years ago—these predators have been stomping on others throughout history. The truly dumb are different from leaders who may occasionally do stupid things, make ridiculous requests, or lose their tempers and then, during reflective moments, apologize.

In our consulting work, we have worked with truly dumb bosses. Yet each time we interview someone and discover another, and then another, we wonder. As much as we think we understand, we are still dumbfounded.

How do such people get into positions of authority, and once there, what sustains them? Historians, biographers, and social scientists have all looked at those questions. For these specialists, the phenomenon we've termed "truly dumb" is taken very seriously. Because when we move beyond the workplace and look at "dumbness" as part of the whole of human experience, it can translate into something quite frightening.

In the workplace, what can be driving such irrational, insensitive bosses? Are they misinterpreting the words and intentions of their employees? Are they unaffected by the feelings of others because they cannot experience their own? Do they need to confirm their uniqueness by denying the individuality of their staff? In *Manufacturing Social Distress: Psychopathy in Everyday Life,* Robert J. Rieber, a distinguished jurist at John Jay College of Criminal Justice, City University of New York, proposes what he refers to as a "completely new discipline—the psychology of malefaction"—the role of evil in human behavior. Such a discipline comes close to what we've been describing, on a smaller scale, that dumbness at work deserves as serious a study as smartness. The core question raised by Rieber is to what degree persons must be responsible for, and held accountable for, their actions. That question can be equally valid in the workplace. Yet at work, it seems as though the truly dumb boss is seldom reprimanded or held accountable.

LESSON

If you're comfortable working for a dumb boss, it may be because you've been anaesthetized by the drip, drip, drip of daily hurts and insults.

LOVE MY COMPANY, HATE MY MANAGER

Why would Winston, a literate and gregarious man, put up with an arbitrary and insensitive manager for more than a decade? Why would the company want to keep such a manager? Winston describes how he grapples and copes with this type of leadership. He himself is driven to getting his kicks in strange ways.

Winston is an associate editor for a newsletter publisher, a happy and well-spoken man in his forties. We're interviewing him at his company in San Francisco, a high-rise near the financial district. The conference room is in a secluded corner on the visitor's floor in this organization with a reputation for enlightened management. Winston, eyes shining, speaks melodically and sweeps you up with his enthusiasm. Names and places have been changed.

I'll be specific and I'll tell you about one person who's made my life almost absolutely miserable here. It's my boss, the managing editor. She always seems to be trying to impress upper management by cutting costs.

Here's an example, and this is nothing that affected me personally because I work differently than the way my colleagues do. I work faster; I work better by myself. My colleagues rely on support staff, and that's where I'm going with this story.

We were without an editorial assistant in the department for 2 years. The managing editor wouldn't hire one because she thought she was impressing the next level of management—saving a salary. She's constantly telling us, "Remember to cut costs, cut costs."

Finally, on behalf of my colleagues, I took the initiative. I went to the big boss and said, "We've been without an assistant." Me, the one who didn't really need the help, went and asked for it. She finally hired someone. All it took was for me to speak up.

My colleagues complained among themselves, but there's this fear that if they complained out loud, something horrible would happen. The sky would turn red. I don't have that fear. And I find that not only here but in other companies as well. People just don't want to speak up when there is a problem. I tend to run off at the mouth a lot and will speak up. And I sometimes regret what I've done and said. I make an impression—you always do when you speak up—and sometimes I do it before I think.

I wasn't scared because I had gone to personnel to complain about the managing editor in the past and thought that at least I had personnel behind me if my boss got angry. The department needed an assistant, and I was ready to speak up.

Here's another incident. One of my colleagues, Ruth, her husband passed away suddenly. It was a horrible thing. Ruth surprised us all by coming back to work a week after it happened. We worried that she might have a breakdown, and we were all going to have to go out there and rally around her at least. She came back a week later and was able to get flex hours, and she got a lot of attention, which she deserved, having gone through a tragedy like that.

After 3 months, the managing editor called her in and said, "It's been 3 months now since your husband passed away. I think you should be back 100 percent." That's exactly what she said.

These are private matters. Whenever something like this happens, it always seems to get suppressed and nobody really knows about it. Or if people do know, they don't talk about it. It's hushed and it's forgotten the next week completely. There's that fear factor.

This kind of thing happens a lot. Why I've been here for so long I don't know. Complacency, maybe. You want to hear of a really bizarre incident that happened at a meeting? This is great. We were at a meeting, I think 10 or 15 of us, some kind of inter-interdepartmental meeting. We were sitting around this little table. And something occurred to me that made me smile. And I was just slightly smiling and the managing editor stopped and yelled, "What are you smiling at?" I looked at her and didn't know what to say. So I said something innocuous like, "I don't know. I always smile like that." And she said, "Well, stop it. It's very disconcerting." Which was the buzzword for the next week. I would meet people in the halls and say, "You're very disconcerting." It was a joke. It was unbelievable.

But I was very resentful and I almost walked out that day. I was just short of doing that and going right to personnel. I did go to personnel after the meeting. Humiliated is too strong a word because I knew everybody at the meeting and everybody there knew what she was about. They know, but again, nobody says anything.

An edict has gone around recently here, and I think it's overly exaggerated. But if you're caught playing a computer game, you're supposed to be fired on the spot. Pass by *her* office any given time and there's solitaire going—solitaire on the computer most of the day.

But for some reason she's Teflon. They do not see her doing this. I mean, I have taken the games that have come with Microsoft Windows off my computer. I've also taken my sound card out and all that stuff for fear that, you know, I'm going to get caught turning my computer on and it's going to say "welcome" or something like that and the director will be passing by. "You're playing a game." Because I've heard if he sees a graphic he doesn't understand, he assumes that you're playing a game. But it's amazing, she's constantly playing solitaire and never gets caught. I will not go over to the director and say, "Hey, did you know that she's playing solitaire?" It's so funny. If she caught me doing something like this, I would be reprimanded. I'd hear about it for a week.

My impression is that management believes basically she's harmless. It's okay. We can get by with what she does over there. You know, the minimal. As long as her staff keeps working. Which we do. Somehow she gets by.

You become a different person around her. We talk about this woman behind her back. How horrible it is; how she's incompetent. And yet when we talk to her about projects and stuff, "Yes, Sabina. Yes, Sabina. Yes, Sabina." [makes primpy face]

We become different people when we talk to her. I've often said that I will not, that I'm going to go in there and stand up, but I just wimp out completely. I don't hate myself. I don't like that I'm too wimpy, that I can't stand up. You know something? I don't know that I'm afraid. If she has a problem with me, I don't think she would go to personnel, because I think she knows personnel is not her friend. A lot of people are on to her.

There's complacency. I'm fine here with the raises that I get every year. I'm okay. And I have another career that I can go to. But I choose not to, because I'm making money at both right now. I truly like this company. I love it here. I just want her job.

MEANINGS AND LESSONS

Winston tolerates abuse. He knows better. His story reflects a theme you will hear about again: employees who suffer but stay. Suffering and staying are how life is lived at work. It's normal, and the yearning to get out, to find and do better, is what propels the huge self-help market. Some find release in movie-induced fantasies, spectator sports, talk shows, sitcoms, comic strips, and even drugs.

Acceptance, passivity, fear, and organizational nonchalance are what Winston describes. He's showing us an idiotic work environment where bright people permit themselves to be poked, provoked, and pinpricked mercilessly.

He's an engaging man with tremendous energy and high social skills. He's insightful, too, admitting that his behavior in front of his boss is a form of "wimping out." Why is he taking it in spite of his manager's treatment of her staff? He says he has compensating activities—another part-time career affording him gratification—and he likes the money. He enjoys the role of office charmer. He works fast and needs little help. Most important, he claims to love the company. How? Why? For what reasons?

Loving the company is like saying, "I love my family in spite of its faults." The company is his family, and even though a decade has passed during which time the manager he ridicules has been sitting on his head, he accepts her position as a fixture in his corporate family. Sabina's role is the protected mean sibling who gets away with "murder" (computer games etc.) for which others could be fired.

Winston admits to shooting his mouth off at meetings, going above Sabina to her boss, and developing a conspiratorial-like relationship with the personnel department. Yet nothing seems to happen to him, the mouthy, likeable charmer of the group.

LESSON

If you hate your boss, love your company, and stay in spite of everything, then you're not a victim; you're a participant.

What's the game in this white-collar environment? Poor management practice persists in spite of information going up the ladder. In critical ways, the director and Sabina are the same under the skin, motivated to cut costs and keep a tight rein over employees. These educated people are at the center of information-age products—material for companies interested in leading-edge principles. The clue to the game? Gotcha! Winston provides it when he tells of the edict about computer games misinterpreted by management.

LESSON

If your whistle-blowing tendencies are tolerated, it's because they're getting more out of you than you think. You're not winning; you're losing.

SAVAGE MANAGEMENT

Let's take a look at Ruth, the woman whose husband died unexpectedly. Ruth isn't weak. She's a resilient professional and compulsive about work. She doesn't need policing, yet she, like Winston, suffers from the same "dumb" management. Here's her view and analysis. Considerate, compassionate, a decent and somewhat fragile-looking woman, she wanted to share her experiences in spite of some apprehension. She speaks quietly. Names and places have been changed.

I have found in my company that there is not always an ability to practice what is preached. For an organization that believes it has achieved very good management practices, and for the type of organization that it is, it really should.

We have published a number of articles on being a better manager. They've talked about the need for compassion and flexibility, yet I don't think there is any attempt to evaluate those kinds of characteristics in our actual managers. Some managers in this company are flexible and are compassionate and do function as mentors or therapists, not in the clinical sense, but in the way they relate to their subordinates, and others do not. That's been a huge disappointment to me.

I think what I'm trying to say is maybe the culture or the powers that be are not clearly saying to the manager, "It's important for you to sit down and work with your people." The culture is simply saying, "Get the product out quickly, efficiently, and make it of good quality."

Who's to say that because you publish something that means you have to be it? Sure, you're going to publish controversial material, and the company culture is not always going to agree with that. And that's good; that's healthy. This is a democracy; we should have different ideas and approaches. But I think that when . . . Here's another example.

We have published a number of newsletters on the flexible workplace. I always worked 9 to 5 and sometimes stayed late. I'm exempt from overtime. But my husband passed away and it was very, very sudden. And I found that I had trouble sleeping. Sometimes I found that I would wake up early and be very agitated, and I went back to work full time a week after my husband's funeral. And at that time [voice shaking], when I found I was having these problems with insomnia, I requested that I be able to come in at 9:30 and work till 5:30 or beyond, if necessary, to meet my deadlines.

My supervisor, Sabina, who can be very, very inflexible, said to me, "I would prefer that this be a temporary arrangement for only a few months and then I would like you to start coming in at nine o'clock again."

She gave me no reason why nine o'clock was essential. I think it was certainly understood that if there was to be an early morning meeting, I would come in on that day at nine o'clock. I had told her that on the mornings I woke up agitated I had taken to jogging around a nearby park. I would need a little extra time to shower and that half-hour leeway gave me that opportunity. Her response was, "But you won't be jogging come wintertime." My husband passed away in the summer. "So, you won't need the 9:30 then if that's your reason."

I felt that I had been treated as an object. I felt that I was a robot that was supposed to recover from the death of my husband—the sudden death of my husband—within a couple of months and be able to do exactly what everyone else was doing. Except that it wasn't true that everyone else was doing that. In different departments, I knew—and I presume my supervisor knew—that people were working different schedules. That all these kinds of things were going on and I felt that my years with the company counted for nothing; my loyalty and dedication to the company counted for nothing.

An incident happened many months later, and I finally brought out to her not only that issue but other insensitive things that were done when I came back to work after my husband died. I also said something at that time that was perhaps not entirely true, but I felt I had to somehow smooth this after I finally got out other things that were insensitively handled about his death. "Look," I said, "this is a good thing that we're talking this out because we can be honest. We can start our relationship again. We can work on our relationship, much as you'd work on any relationship in your life, husband, wife, sibling, you name it."

And I'm not sure if that was entirely true or not, but it seemed like a positive way for me to couch the words that were exchanged. Word had gotten to her—and how I don't think is important—that I had been venting to certain people in the company about things that had been said and done after my husband's death and my prompt return to work. Something got back to her and she called me into her office and that is when this happened.

Another instance of this sort of robotic approach to management occurred about 3 months after my return to work. I had vacation time coming to me and I gave at least a week's notice that I would like to take all of 6 business days off. I was going to go to a special place for women for a few days. And then I was booking myself into a small hotel and I was going to go on my "retreat." I needed to get away from everyone and everything. There were numerous stresses on me of which she was aware. My late husband's father was dying. She did not want to give me the vacation time because she felt it was a busy time and I was needed to complete projects here. I insisted and I took that time. I simply went around and told everyone I'm going on vacation for 6 days; she didn't come out and say, "I forbid it." But she said, "You really shouldn't; this is a bad time. There are projects. There [visibly shaken and agitated voice] are deadlines. Can't you do it another time?" This was 3 months after he died.

[in a raspy, loud voice] "There are projects. The projects are important. We have to get these things in on time!" I tend to be always nervous about my job; that's just my own nature. I was not scared of her in any physical way, certainly. But I suppose one always fears for one's job. My anxiety level was high to begin with, and once again I felt I might as well be a number. I think it is so important in an organization that you look at the individual. I think that managers need to have insight into their subordinates and their different reactions. I think that anyone who knows me well thinks I'm practically obsessive about wanting to be really good at what I do. But she didn't seem to think that doing my work well and efficiently and meeting my deadlines are extremely important to me. I am far from a lazy or lackadaisical employee. You need to be able to look at your subordinates as individuals and see that you can probably be harsher with one subordinate, who may be coming in late or doing something wrong, than with another, whom you perceive as doing something wrong or not, understanding the importance of deadlines.

Yes, insensitivity. It's people skills that are so important. And, you know, I hear other stories from people both in our organization and in other organizations. The same sort of mentality exists whereby you expect exactly the same from each of your subordinates who has the same basic position and you don't take personality characteristics into consideration.

I think that the bottom line for this organization, and I doubt it's alone, is if we're doing better financially, then our managers must be doing enough right. We're not going to worry if we hear an occasional rumor or something filters down to us. And I think that's probably not just here. I have friends who work for different organizations and I'm getting the sense that over the last decade or so, increasingly it's far more important that if you are a profit-making section of the company, they're not going to worry so much about how a department's being run when you're making a profit.

MEANINGS AND LESSONS

We will use Ruth's story to look at two distortions of fair dealing in the social contract between employer and employee and how they sustain dumbness. The first is what this whole book is about: that the free exercise of authority affects employee emotions in more negative ways than society acknowledges. The other is the control over the individual through an abusive use of the *Diagnostic and Statistical Manual of the American Psychiatric Association (DSM-IV)*. It can be a weapon against employees and is a contemporary version of the fifteenth-century codex employed in Spain to define heretics. Here's an example.

Nancy, an office worker, became depressed, couldn't work, and sought the help of a psychiatrist as a result of being denied a promotion she felt she deserved. She sued her employer on the basis of discrimination and emotional distress caused by a deteriorating relationship with her supervisor, a former friend who had been promoted above her. Two psychiatrists, hers and her company's, felt she showed symptoms of paranoid thinking, and both defined her as having a major depressive disorder, single episode, unspecified (*DSM-IV* 296.20). She told people she wasn't crazy, but she just couldn't work with her supervisor and would take a comparable position anywhere else in the company. But in the eyes of the establishment, since she was diagnosable, her claim had no merit.

In the *DSM*, all of human behavior can be catalogued in terms of illness. Whoever you are and whatever you might do (there are not many exceptions), the *DSM* will get you. The absurdity of trying to encompass the human condition in a 3-lb, 886-page tome is humorously and incisively explained by L. J. Davis in "The Encyclopedia of Insanity" (*Harper's Magazine*, February 1997):

> This in the end is the beauty of the *DSM-IV*. Hangnails seem to have avoided the amoeba's kiss, and the common cold is momentarily safe (unless it is accompanied by pain), but precious little else...If every aspect of human life (excepting, of course, the practice of psychiatry) can be read as pathology, then everything human beings thought they knew, believed, or deduced about their world is consigned to the dustbin of history or a line on an insurance form.

Returning to Ruth. After the unexpected death of her husband, Sabina moved into the center of Ruth's consciousness. How could a manager with whom no relationship existed outside of work become so meaningful? It starts in petty ways affecting all of Ruth's colleagues. But then, after the death of her husband, Sabina's legalistic-sounding constraints began defining Ruth to herself and altering her self-perception. Fortunately, trusting Ruth became defiant and took a week off. To remain sane in the crazy environment, Ruth had to redefine herself in her own terms, not in Sabina's. Compared to Nancy, whose work problems needed the intervention of psychiatry, Ruth kept herself beyond the reach of the inquisitors. Ruth might have been judged to have paranoid thoughts about her boss if she had fallen into the wrong hands. She remained on the job and had the insight to know that a long period of mourning away from work might have jeopardized her career. She knew her enemy.

═══════════════════════════════════════

LESSON
When you act "tough" and protect your center, they'll be less inclined to take advantage of you.

═══════════════════════════════════════

The negative energy in Ruth's workplace comes, in large part, from her boss. Arrayed against that energy are Ruth's love of work, which she performs conscientiously, a supportive group of colleagues, and a high degree of self-sufficiency and self-respect.

LESSON

To keep from being dragged in the dirt by tyrants, know that the problem is with them, not with you, or with how you do your job.

BIG MAN WITH A BAT

Boom-boom-boom-boom, faster and faster beat the drums inside the Roman galleon. "Ram speed. Keep them in chains," cried the captain. "Ram now!" Here's a contemporary version of that movie scene. Not a galleon, but a brokerage office. Ron, a baby boomer, fit and competent looking, is a stockbroker and has been in the business for 25 years. He sits quietly with hands clasped on his lap and looks straight ahead. He is too timid—almost shy, we think—for the on-top-of-it job he must have in business for himself. All of that changes when he speaks. Then we see he is polite and considerate, not timid at all. He is well-mannered. Names and places have been changed.

> The craziest I ever met was a manager I had who was with Ross, Shaw, Herbert. I was with Roberts, and after Ross bought them, they consolidated all their offices out here under one man, the former Ross manager. It went to his head. He thought that since he took over three offices in town, he was now the big shot and was in control.
>
> Really he was just lucky, in the right place at the right time. He was a lot luckier than he was smart.
>
> In the brokerage, this guy managed by intimidation. He was a couple of steps removed from the cave. He would come out on the last day of every production month with a Louisville Slugger bat, and

he'd go from office to office, from desk to desk. He'd have the brokers put their hands out on the edge of their desks, and then he'd
take that baseball bat [makes a mock swing down on the dining
room table, ending in a loud crash] and swing as hard as he could
on the edge of your desk.

I'm serious. And he'd say, "Are you going to get me $10,000 in
commissions today?" The bat was lying on the desk and I'd say, "I
don't know, John. I'll try." And he'd say, "Put your hand out there
again, a little closer to the edge." *Bang!* went the bat. He said, I'll
come back and I'd better have at least $5000 in commissions today."
And that was the man's style and that's how he liked to get production out of his people.

We had things we'd like to do with that baseball bat to him.
[laughs] Now I can laugh. After his little performance, nobody was
going to help him out. He got his just desserts, but that was later.
Meantime, he was promoted and moved up, made regional vice
president. Then he could go around and talk to all the managers. I
suppose he took his bat with him.

He was very political and he was maneuvering and always
climbing the ladder. He had a different persona around management
[makes a mincing face] than he did around the people he super-
vised. He probably got promoted because his production went up so
high because of the merging of the three offices. On paper, his numbers went way up. But it did catch up with him. After he was promoted, he fell on bad times. People didn't tolerate his style well, and
I heard he was demoted back to a small branch, and then they didn't
like him in that branch, so he got put in a central city office in a bad
neighborhood. I don't know what became of the guy. He was not
well thought of, but he was a Louisville Slugger.

One man committed suicide. It had a lot to do with the job. It
happened at work. He overdosed at work, signed out, went home,
and died in 2 hours. That is the worst example of what one person
can do to another.

I stayed for a year and a half. And what happened to that
successful office, the most successful in the city? Two or three of
the twenty-five brokers stayed in the business and everybody
else left.

MEANINGS AND LESSONS

There are "slugger" elements within many managers who've never been taught an alternative to the bully-as-winner model. Most of those tendencies are kept under wraps. Ron's story is sick. Motivating with a bat is a scene that could have been fictionalized for a movie or play, and few would have thought it unusual. This explains a great deal about how dumbness verges into greed into power and sometimes into a jail sentence.

We're dealing with what today reads like an exaggeration of reality. But recall the period, the mid-1980s, times of mergers, wholesale downsizings, and vast changes in the financial industry. Hubris everywhere. Whatever fantasies Ron's broker colleagues had—the stuff of bad dreams—the monster of childhood had miraculously appeared. *Crash!* went the bat. Up surged the adrenalin, but there was no place to run. The monster, at least Ron thinks so, slew one man and stampeded twenty-two others. Then the monster was transferred—buried, to continue the metaphor—to a risky inner city neighborhood. End of trail.

LESSON

Beware of managers with bats. They will steal your accomplishments as they steal your self-respect.

Stories like these raise questions worth a deeper look (we saw it in the lives of Winston and Ruth): Why do people stay so long and what is it doing to them? Ron lived more than a year with the crack of the bat, but he can't explain why. Nobody complained. The numbers were against them and in the brokerage business numbers are everything. That's the clue in Ron's case—numbers. Numbers define the mythology of power and the alpha (Ron's manager) touched by it becomes momentarily magical. The alpha has to be unmasked and unseated, which ultimately happened. The employees waited;

there was little else they could do, and finally life paid back the slugger. Ron is convinced that one broker was driven to suicide. However, there may be more to the story than he knows. What, finally, are we shown about Ron's "successful" office? Employees were helpless in the face of unsurmountable odds. It was a system that could look a dollar sign straight in the face yet had to avert its gaze when the face became a human one.

=====

LESSON

When your boss averts his gaze, it's because a big surprise may be in the works, one you probably won't like.

=====

CAN'T TALK, WORKING ON THE PHONES

There's a classic skit of the compulsive host who during a lively party runs around emptying ashtrays, wiping and tidying up, unconcerned and oblivious to events happening around her. In this story, you'll meet a similar type, the manager who compulsively installs computer and phone terminals as his employees conduct the business of his bank. This misfit manager story comes courtesy of Julie and Jennie, who lived it. They are in their forties and have known each other for more than 20 years. They compete over who's going to speak first as they relate outlandish episodes. We are in our offices. Names and places have been changed.

JULIE: Jennie and I both worked for Willie in Dallas at BankThree. They were really good to their employees until they got too big.

JENNIE: And then they stole all the money. They were years ahead of themselves.[laughs] No, really, extremely ahead of themselves in training. You were always in training and we were trained for the whole picture, not just one segment of it.

JULIE: The bank was doing it the right way, and in a very short time, they were worth a ton of money. They made a separate mortgage division and then had the vision to seek secondary loans, get their money back, take the fee for servicing, and . . .

JENNIE: Round and round it went, over and over again. And the stock went up. We were better paid than anyone else in the industry, and the knowledge we gained was phenomenal.

JULIE: They had a management training program, but unfortunately, they put people into it who were maybe good talkers but were not good managers. That's where Willie came in. He was our manager; he dumped on us. He was on the ceiling one day and on the floor the next. And you never knew what was going on or what he would try to do. He was a screamer; he was everything. The only way we survived was because Jennie and I ran the office.

JENNIE: We made all the decisions; we did everything. He rewired the place. He would come in and be in a depressive mood. He had worked at a theme park as a telephone person, so he decided that we needed more telephone outlets. He would go through the whole office installing four telephone outlets in each office.

JULIE: He thought we needed more telephone contact. He put in intercom systems, he rewired things, he did anything to avoid dealing with the operation of the bank.

JENNIE: We did nothing to hurt him. We accepted him the way he was but knew he was doomed from day one. After about a year, he was gone.

JULIE: He was without a doubt the worst manager—the worst person in terms of any kind of leadership.

JENNIE: He would put in new computer things. It would drive you absolutely crazy if you let it. But luckily, he left us alone to run the show. We were there from seven in the morning to seven at night if we didn't have a party.

JULIE: Oh yeah, we had PR (public relations) parties. He was big into PR. He would stage these PR parties and then leave. He was never at anything. He had the worst personality and it's very difficult, if not impossible, to deal with someone like that. He could come in the morning and be the happiest person and by the afternoon just walk around and throw things off the desks and scream at the women who were working at the desks. And walk in and slam the vault or take the money out of the vault—"This isn't put in right!"—and take it all out, sometimes in front of the customers. He was absolutely nutso.

JENNIE: He got a divorce. He got remarried and then divorced. The last time I saw him, he had a beard down to here. He had a very pleasant personality as long as he was up. And when he wasn't up, it was the worst thing. You never knew. He could walk in and say, "Let's have a party . . . let's do lunch." And he'd go out and buy the stuff for lunch and then by lunchtime he hated all of us. He wouldn't come in the kitchen.

JULIE: He was being backstabbed by one of the vice presidents. He knew it, but there was nothing he could do about it. It drove him nuts. Jennie and I ran the whole thing and he got the credit. Never gave anybody any credit for anything. He was in a position where he didn't belong. Should have stayed at the theme park working on telephones.

JENNIE: In their infinite wisdom his bosses said, "Willie, you're just not happy over here; we're going to transfer you." They put him in a management position in Fort Worth. That was after we finally complained that it had to stop. The VP came over to our branch and said, "I have to tell him that you talked." Squealed more or less. People were walking out and you couldn't blame them. You can't run the bank without people.

JULIE: So the VP comes in—he was such a doll—puts his briefcase down, and says, "I'll be out in a few minutes." Talks to Willie for 3 minutes in the kitchen, comes out, says everything's okay, and leaves. Talk about wanting to crawl under a desk somewhere. My God. Well, I got busy.

JENNIE: Then Willie walks in just before his time to leave. Of course, we never got to leave. He said, "Jennie I need to talk to you." I said, "Yes, Willie." He said, "I want to thank you." "You do?" He said, "I know I was wrong. I owe you an apology." I said, "You don't owe me anything. You owe those women an apology." The next morning, he didn't come in to work, if that's what you can call it. He just held a meeting and said he felt he was a jerk and he was sorry. Did he mean it? *No!* That's when they transferred him out. They shipped him to Fort Worth.

JULIE: He continued the same style there and he only lasted 6 months.

MEANINGS AND LESSONS

Julie and Jennie ran a branch bank for a completely inept, no business- and no people-skills manager. They describe some-one who had no conception of what it means to manage, who had been given training but had no capacity or desire to learn. They coped by doing their boss's job, not because they were protecting him—he was a jerk in their eyes—but because they seized a tremendous learning opportunity. The banking opera-tion of which they were a part easily overrode Willie's nega-tive effects. They took the opportunity and profited by it. Ultimately, they had to blow the whistle as Willie's behavior became even more bizarre, some episodes taking place in front of customers.

LESSON
It's worth remaining in a learning environment even though your immediate boss is dumb.

Picture Willie putting in phone lines and computer termi-nals oblivious to the bank business swirling around him. Picture the two women, like three-armed paperhangers doing theirs and Willie's work—gobbling up ideas for their later careers. That's comedic, and readily grasped.

What is craziest, however, is Willie's selection in the first place. The women explain that he made a positive impression, well and good. The bank's expansion mode and need for managers are also understandable. What they can't explain is how anyone in their right-personnel minds could think that a theme park telephone operator qualified for a bank manager's job. But there is a clue.

It's the very culture of the bank itself. It's making so much money so quickly, awash in it, in fact, and letting its tremen-dous success obliterate the need for good judgment in person-nel. It simply didn't matter that much, and that's what appears to have affected the thinking of the human resources people.

The people at the top weren't watching the store. They were too busy stealing money, the women say. The system became larcenous.

===

LESSON

If you're left alone at work, you can become as smart or dumb as you please.

===

THE MORALE SURVEY AS BEAUTY CONTEST

You need votes to stay in power. You get votes by distorting survey results. In this Fortune 100 corporation, top managers stayed in power and looked good by playing with "objective" morale survey results. But why should that surprise you? After all, it's their company, their surveys, and their manager of quality. The story is told by Frank, the supposedly "independent" manager of quality. There is nothing wishy-washy about this man in his midforties. Frank is direct and somewhat gruff. He'd be a tough act to follow were he to ditch his employer.

He knows his employer well, having come up through the ranks, working in production and administration. As a trained engineer, he knows how his leaders and operating people think. He didn't want to speak in his office so we met at noon, enveloped by the noise of the city, and sat on a bench in his company's beautiful raised patio.

Frank is sincere when he says his feelings of loyalty to the *idea* of his company are high. But his sense of betrayal by an administration he cannot respect is predominant. Names and places have been changed.

> It was January 2, the first day back after the holidays. And the situation is my buddy and I come back, talking about family events, all that kind of nice stuff, and exchanging, "Hey, how're you doing?" Just general small talk. Socialization. We're partners in crime, so to speak, in trying to do the right things in this business. In walks our senior executive vice president. Now, he does not occupy this area;

he lives in the stratosphere. And he rarely comes down here, but this is the first day of work so he walks down the floor and comes over to us. He says, "What are you guys doing? Why aren't you working on that survey? You're lowering our scores."

To put that in perspective, it's an employee feedback system, and we weren't looking too good. It's a classic story of passing out the ballots, collecting the votes, and never telling the employees who won the election. He was irritated at the fact that they were a little low. Well, don't pass out the ballots if you're not willing to hear bad news and take some action. That gives him a black mark on his scorecard. The scores are supposed to help us improve the performance of the employee base.

But now we're starting to use them, I would say, as clubs to beat over the heads of certain executives for not doing the right thing. It should be used as a learning tool. But they get nothing, no feedback from the management. Employees are telling us, "You guys keep asking us for feedback, but we never see any action as a result of our feedback. What do you want us to do, keep answering the same question until we give you the right answer?"

It was one of those things that have transpired over several years here that has basically made me lose confidence in the seniormost management of this company. One of the things I asked them is, "What are the assets we have that our competitors do not and cannot duplicate?" And so they say, "Well, we've got capital and technology." So I say, "Our competitors have research capabilities too, and they develop technology and they have capital—so where is the competitive advantage?"

The answer is people. And most of the management has yet to come up with that answer. Now, people in themselves are not the whole answer. It's how people are managed and the systems that support them. And they have yet to figure that out.

MEANINGS AND LESSONS

Frank didn't know how lucky he might be, observing the possible disappearance of a maladaptive organization. What tales he could tell later in retirement, sitting with friends at a country club. That prospect wasn't on his mind today. Our conversation provoked him to look at what he could see as the downfall of his company as he knew it. According to his analysis, things couldn't get much worse.

Frank's story allows us to look at one of an organization's most important cultural engines—trust. Trust is an engine that (1) may work smooth as silk, (2) may work well in fits and starts depending on circumstances, (3) may groan and sputter like the worn-out ship's engine in the Bogart-Hepburn movie *The African Queen,* or (4) may be dead in the water.

We know this. Frank doesn't trust his boss in general nor his boss's insight. His boss, a high-status example of the company's management style, doesn't trust employees and shows them no respect. Frank's company falls between alternatives (3) and (4).

LESSON

If your leader has little respect for those under you, it's certain he or she has little respect for you.

The story begins with what can be called a "gem of dumbness." The beginning of a new year, a seldom visited site where Frank and his friend work, and an opportunity for management to communicate a human, caring message. Instead, as if the people he's complaining to don't breathe, bleed, and experience joy and sadness as he does, the boss thinks only of himself. It's an example of gross insensitivity coupled with a gluttonous narcissism. ("I want you to consider me, me, me and nothing else, and how I'll look!")

LESSON

Selfish leaders' careers are always in danger. Peers hate them. Top level executives don't trust them. Subordinates are out for revenge.

The company uses a standard form complete with national norms. The instrument looks carefully wrought, sincere, and honest—if any survey of that sort can be described that way with a straight face. Frank's respondents, most of the 3000+ employees, as he tells it, didn't have a straight face. They had angry and suspicious faces. Obviously, the survey had nothing at all to do with its ostensible purpose. It was nothing more than a piece of corporate debris spun around by a tornadolike suction created by top managers who want everything on their terms.

LESSON

It's not your imagination when you feel pulled against your will into the vortex of corporate policy. It's management's way of telling you who has the power.

MBA—MANAGEMENT BY ADULTERY

This story proves what many suspect: that under the right circumstances, dumb adultery can pay. Meaning you can have your cake and eat it, too. You might think that an adulterous relationship is usually a catastrophe waiting to happen. Not always, as Happy, the woman you're about to meet, will show you.

Happy is a loan officer and talking with us in her office in Milwaukee, Wisconsin. She is 45 and strikingly handsome. She smiles and laughs readily. In the rural community where she grew up, it would be said, "That girl doesn't have a mean bone in her body, but she's mouthy." And yes, she was, but in the positive sense. She's married to a lawyer and has two grown children. Names and places have been changed.

> I've mostly worked for smaller organizations. If there was a problem in other companies, I was always able to have a voice in saying something.
>
> I can tell you I had a situation where I worked for 6 years. I was the director of marketing and I was out selling the business and how good it was. In the meantime, my boss was having an affair with one of the people in the office. I was about the last one to know, but everybody else in the office knew and it cut the morale down so

badly that the work was bad. And I'm out there selling the best company in town not knowing that the work is coming out real badly and all the things that were going on.

I was selling title insurance. You sell the service to attorneys, builders, bankers; that's how I got to know so many people in the industry. I would talk to them, entertain them, build relationships with them. I promised them excellent service, quick work, accuracy. I was out all the time, so I didn't see it plus I don't see stuff like that until it hits me right in the face. When your president is fooling with somebody else in the company and going for 3-hour lunches and whatever, the whole morale in the company fell apart and people just didn't care anymore.

And it actually got out into the community, you know, with the realtors and builders saying, "Hey, what's going on with your boss?" So people in the industry started knowing about it. It was really a tough situation, and I confronted him with it, too, as well as other people in the office by saying, "Hey, here's what these people are saying about you. Is this true?" And he continues to deny it. But he continued to take 3–4-hour lunches with this person, getting caught in the office a couple times and having the wife storm in a couple times. The whole place was just very disruptive.

It was one of those 150-year-old businesses. People were there for many, many years, and this person came in. He was a young attorney of 45 and became president and one-third owner. The two other owners had different businesses entirely; they were just investors. They left him alone to run it.

Well, eventually I had to leave. It broke my heart because my heart was in the job, and going out and trying to do a good job and not being backed up by the company in the performance was really tough and then it was such a personal thing. I really liked the guy. We were friends, too. But I felt bad. I knew his wife, too, and you don't want to be in the middle of situations like that, when the wife would come in looking for him or calling for him. But still, that's very disruptive for work.

If you're going to have an affair, do it outside the office. Or do it behind other people's eyes. They really pretty much flaunted it. There's no way people didn't know it, and if nothing else, I said to him, "You just don't treat any employee more special than another one." You know, going out for 3-hour lunches is not acceptable behavior. People were working their butts off doing their work and they see this other woman who's in the same category as they are running off with the boss for 3 or 4 hours getting special treatment.

And when they're gone, don't you think—knowing those two are off for a while—that people are going to take advantage of the time? If these guys are out screwing around, why shouldn't we be screwing around? No one ever got in trouble for anything. No one ever got reprimanded for anything. I'd come back with complaints, and I think they pretty much fell by the wayside.

Title insurance is the kind of insurance where you shouldn't have any claims. It's very meticulous work, and they'd miss stuff or they'd miss deadlines.

I think the emotion might have been not being appreciated for their work more than anything. Maybe they were angry because somebody that worked right next to them didn't have to work as hard as they did. There were some who took advantage of it and some that didn't. What they would do is not meet deadlines, which was more severe really. In the title insurance business, the prices are all set by the insurance commissioner, so the competitiveness isn't necessarily the price, it's the service. It's more how fast you can get things out. You know.

He promoted his mistress to manager of the title department. And I said to him, "Well, you know, even I have never gone out for long lunches like that and I'm your director of marketing. I'm the one, you know, you should be bouncing all this stuff off of." And his mistress was also married. They would put in a lot of extra time at the office, and people would come in and find beer cans and alcohol stuff.

He was the president and owner. What were they going to do, fire him? And no one ever told the other owners.

It's been 2 years since I left, and the affair is still going on. Their reputation is not good. They still get some business because the owner also has a relationship with an owner of a real estate firm. They are big drinking buddies, and this owner is an adulterer, too. They kind of all follow in that same kind of crowd. Yeah.

No, it doesn't shock me but it disappoints me, mostly because it affected me in my business. I was out selling something that I thought was a good thing and I'm out there trying to get people to use this company because I think it's the best and that activity in the company wasn't backing me up. It was enough to make me leave. I used to say if I didn't have to get paid, I would still do it anyway because I liked it so much. You know.

MEANINGS AND LESSONS

Happy's president has something on most office Romeos. He continues to get away with it, flaunting it in public, and daring his staff and his wife to do anything. It's not a good model for little boys in Milwaukee growing up poor and MBA and LLB students at The University of Wisconsin, Madison and Milwaukee.

Happy documents mistakes and reduced productivity. She tells how the old firm's good name became tarnished. You would think those items would be enough to force any enterprise out of business. But more was involved than the free market.

LESSON

A free market in adultery, and other socially unacceptable behaviors, can only exist when the boss has absolute power.

Notice that low morale and mistakes are not tied to big issues: personal values or ethics. They're tied to little things like office favoritism, long lunch hours, and the elevation of the girlfriend to manager. Happy felt pushed aside. It was she who should have been consulted on marketing matters. The affair was an open secret. Does that plot sound familiar?

LESSON

When your boss tramples on convention, don't act the abused child. Do your job and make your move when it suits you.

Happy likes her president in spite of her indignation and the public embarrassment of dangling in the marketplace making promises that couldn't be fulfilled. She quits. If only he would be more discreet, not parade it, and not do it within the industry, says Happy. What's all that about? It's the need to connect to him, the respect for him in spite of everything, and the psychic mentoring attachment to the top.

There is a sex and power story here beyond what Happy talks about. Consensual sex in the office is one end of the scale; the other is true sexual harassment. The president uses his position of authority and hits on a young married woman. She buys the deal and gets rewarded. The lovers (?) wave victory flags and leave mementos all over the office. There are no statistics about office affairs that pay off. In other versions, the president hits on a female employee who doesn't buy it. She sues and the case may go to trial. There are no flags or mementos there, unless you want to include red ones of danger.

I'M ALPHA, YOU'RE DIRT

Control—emotional, spiritual, and economic. Meet a one-man punk band. If you don't like his music, get out. This story about a company in the training industry will make you think of a horror movie. Madelene, the young woman talking to us, is an independent film producer. We're at a popular restaurant in the Soho section of New York. It's after lunch. Male and female boomers in suits, Xers in sweaters and jeans, and that rainbow category of beautifully dressed young women have mostly gone. Madelene is attractive and electric. Her eyes flash as she speaks, moving both hands for emphasis and in rhythm with her sentences. She's a take-charge, fast-speaking, means-business person. Her laughter is contagious. She cut her teeth in broadcasting and now handles major projects for Fortune 100 and 500 companies. Names and places have been changed.

> It was a bizarre, entertainment-world culture. An extremely macho, but frightened, man ran the company. If he had the slightest hesitation about somebody, he would fire them. He didn't trust his own instincts; that was my assumption because he wasn't well schooled and he came out of sales, not out of entertainment. Because he didn't trust his own instincts, he didn't trust other people's either. If he liked

your idea, it had to be along his own line of thinking. So basically, unless you were a member of his style of culture, you were never going to make it there.

The case is that most people couldn't make it there. Every day someone was fired. And for a company with only about 40 people, that's really a lot of people to either distrust or decide that they're not good enough or something.

The first moment I met him, I knew there was something awry. You walk into his office and everything is black. A big black table. Pan up. He's a guy wearing an open shirt with gold medallions hanging out over his chest. Pan up further and you see gray hair and a very obvious toupee, smoking a stogy and drinking a cocktail. This is the middle of the day. So walking in there was like walking into some macho playboy-of-the-60s type den.

At that time, 1991, the job market was very, very tight. He could always find somebody, despite the culture, to come in and take a job. It was my experience that when I told people I had a job there, they would look at me, like, "oh." And they'd look at me like there was something I didn't know. Apparently, everybody knew that it was this type of culture industrywide.

They leaned very heavily on a few well-known talents, names everyone would surely know, big names in business. And they were always afraid of their relationship with those people. Frightened about how many years of profitability remained. Tapes are expensive to make. Always looking for new people. They had big names but not a lot of product. They were beginning to lose market share and really desperate to go find something else to sell. So they began looking for acquisitions, something somebody else had already done for them to distribute.

Only a doormat would fit there. Those were the kind of people that had any staying power. They were doormats intellectually and emotionally. People who were not doormats either left of their own volition or were fired. They would come into conflict with the leader of the company at some point.

In an entrepreneurial venture, the ability to brainstorm a new idea is absolutely essential. And to keep relationships alive is also essential. So if you have fighting amongst the ranks, you don't have a team; you don't have a company.

My worst experience? Yeah, I worked really, really hard on this week-long scout with another producer. And in order to satisfy them, not only did I work 12-hour days, I then had to fly back from California and write that entire time about my experiences. They would never give me a computer, so I had to buy my own. I was absolutely exhausted because it's very hard to stay awake on a plane. But I had a lot of work to get done. I came back and had an 11-page document in which I described four companies and five sites, about a page and a half each. They threw it back in my face and said, "Oh, we could never read all this."

I said, "Well, if you don't want an understanding of what we saw and did, then I don't think we can tell you anything. If you'd like some glossed-over opinion, why don't you ask the other producer who really hasn't done much?"

So I do all the work for her and she shows up and directs, which to me seemed absolutely pointless. From that point forward, I don't feel like working there anymore. The other problem was when I came back, I received a new phone list of extensions on which five or six people I knew were no longer there. I said, "What happened to these people?" [whispers] "Oh, they're all gone now." Well this is almost one sixth of the company. They had all either just left or been fired.

The guy should step down, and he eventually did. No way to salvage him. He was too dark. He was very into himself. His office, his clothing, his demeanor, it was all about satisfying his ego. The vice president of the company was a woman he plucked out of the secretarial staff who was forced to stay in the same hotel room with him. It was frighteningly strange. In order to satisfy him, she would wear slinky clothes to work. She would complain to me, "He's making me do this." And I'd say, "Well, why are you wearing this low-cut outfit?" It was incredibly bizarre—almost as if, if you were a woman, you were expected not to be tough, but be sort of a cheap type to satisfy his needs.

I know that he respected me for my mind and my opinions, but I never met anyone like this before. He was causing the company to run downhill. Nobody could get along with him or his assistant. There was just no esprit de corps. Not a team.

You can't have a guy who's into himself and have a company be a real team. Egomania does not build trust or creative spirit or the passion to drive something forward.

MEANINGS AND LESSONS

This twisted story, told with a sense of the dramatic by an articulate and keen observer, is a unique statement about what we consider to be a nonculture. The element of loyalty is irrelevant. How could there be no culture? There must have been something. We'll explain. Think of a fishing boat that can be chartered for 1-day excursions. There's the boat, the captain, and the paraphernalia that goes with catching fish. Each day, there is a different group of passengers. It would be stretching it to say the boat has a culture, since it's people that make a culture happen. Madelene's company was essentially transient. The "culture" was the quirky personality of the boss.

Loyalty wasn't needed because employees were really freelancers who had an assignment (job) for a time. One person dominated, and everything turned on his perception. He bought what he needed and discarded it when it no longer pleased him. He was, in a small, pathetic way, somewhat like the Roman emperors at the beginning of the Christian era. Employees were moved around at will, obeyed, and were undoubtedly forced to play to the leader's vanity if they could.

When Madelene talks about the impossibility of a team under such conditions, she's absolutely correct. But would teams have made any difference?

She tells us that talented people left because they were demeaned, not respected for their opinions, and were like dirt under their boss's feet. Her choice of the word "doormats" for those who stayed is inspired. We observe the same negative environments that force out the best people. Said another way, smart people leave and dumb people stay.

LESSON

Doormat managers prevent leaders from learning or seeing anything new.

Failure is heaped on failure, inefficiency upon inefficiency, until products lose their quality and competitive advantage.

Loyalty no longer has any role, is no longer the glue or the rallying point. Leaders are ultimately deserted, and if an organization is large enough, they are replaced by boards of directors.

The story raises a troubling question: What kind of relationship is there, if any, between an organization's culture and its product? Don Peterson, in his book explaining Ford's design resurgence (20), tells how the culture inside Ford became more positive, how quality improved, and how unlocking creativity started an industrywide trend of round-shaped cars beginning with the Taurus. When General Motors began the new Saturn culture—participative and enlightened—consumers responded to no-haggle pricing, and a loyal following was born. Saturns receive some of the highest scores for customer satisfaction. How then could the rotten environment described by Madelene have produced such apparently high quality, expensive, and popular business videos?

There is a positive lesson here. Her company represents an instance of what's occurring with greater frequency in creative fields. In graphic design, software, visual arts, and publishing, to name a few, people work independently. They feed their input to a "boss" whom they may seldom see. Transient teams are formed, do their work, and disperse.

LESSON
Empowered people who are loyal to themselves can produce quality work anywhere.

PASTILLE DUMB

A small loaf of dumbness is good for a laugh at the end of a chapter like this. John is in marketing for an airplane manufacturer. He's in his forties, a straight-talking man with twinkling eyes and a wry smile.

> I had a manager who didn't look at results. I don't know, he was strange. He would chew me out for walking around to get my job done. He felt that you should sit at your desk and do your job.

There's no reason to leave your desk. Well, I had to deal with engineers. You can't always find an engineer on the phone. Most of the time, they don't answer the phone. So you would have to go to where the engineers are. Track them down, get the print and the information from them. And I actually got written up on my review for doing my job. To me, I couldn't believe it. It was the first time I got written up for anything. This guy was a new boss. I ended up getting a bad mark on my review for doing my job.

MEANINGS AND LESSONS

How many ways can a boss screw-up? Here's one you might like to add to your list. The humor is black and lies in visualizing the actual scene: "Stay at your desk." "I gotta walk around to do my job." "I don't care. Stay at your desk."

LESSON
You cannot be doing your job even when you are doing your job if your boss says so.

Being on the receiving end of a bad review is serious stuff, and John knows it. That piece of management artillery in the hands of vindictive or just plain dumb bosses is a cursed document and has to be replaced by mutual trust and respect. We said something like that to John, who said what you are now probably thinking, "You've gotta be kidding."

TRULY DUMB ORGANIZATIONS

Managed care, a kind of medical apartheid, has fathered many examples of the dysfunctional organization. In this chapter's anchor interview, "Specialists for Me," a specialist in oncology at a teaching hospital talks for the record and defines this category.

In the truly dumb organization, you always find the fatuous mission statement, the straightjacket policy manual, unproductive strategic planning sessions, and a mostly irrelevant training program. Yet even in such a barren landscape, as cactus holds water to sustain life for those who know how to get it, there are smart subleaders who are ready to slake their employees' thirst for growth. The "Biker Chick," "Genius," and "Insanity" stories are examples of how sustenance can still be provided even in an emotionally deadening organization.

In a truly dumb organization, everyone's wrong except the people at the top. Employee feelings (patients in healthcare organizations) don't really matter. Job insecurity, in spite of strong economic numbers, is felt at all levels. There is little trust. Stress is high. Loyalty is minimal. A survey by International Survey Research of 1000 large companies found that 46 percent of employees worried about being laid off, up from 31 percent in 1992. Within downsized companies, cynicism and mistrust remain. No one believes that stability has returned to corporate life. (*The Wall Street Journal,* July 21, 1997). Something truly dumb is going on. The article recommends the need to build trust. Dream on.

Psychiatry, always on the prowl for new categories of illness, has come to the rescue of some. You may have "layoff survivor sickness." Cigna Insurance and the American Management Association found that workers at companies with cutbacks remained disabled 28 days longer than workers in companies that did not downsize. If you decide to sue for emotional distress, psychiatry is there to help.

Truly dumb organizations are profoundly insensitive to employee mortality. The resulting cynicism among employees is no different from what Paul Fussell writes about in *Wartime* and what Ernie Pyle illustrated about soldiers in World War II. Implications are denied. There is little understanding of consequences. There is even a serious question about actual IQ.

The organizations described in this chapter have that special quality of dense stupidity—the fighter foundering against the ropes, the drunken actor missing cues.

Employees in truly dumb companies become partially immobilized, as if infected with a virus that acts relentlessly inside their bodies. They must live with the virus until they fight it through. Some consciously alienate themselves, trying to protect their core beliefs by pretending they don't even work in the company. Incessantly absurd behavior can sound like a swarm of locusts chattering inside your head. Some respond with heightened activity, go through a symbolic mutiny, and take over operating the company as if their ship of commerce had mysteriously lost all its leaders. A few become poets, philosophers, teachers, or analysts and may write about business either on or off the job. Some may develop the layoff survivor syndrome mentioned earlier and seek out an attorney. Fewer still commit literal or figurative suicide.

SPECIALISTS FOR ME, 15 MINUTES FOR YOU

Marketing staff running hospitals, accountants running research labs, MBAs running clinics, quality assurance managers clocking surgeons, HMO clerks deciding your treatment options. Reservation clerks, who know where the plane's going, flying Concords? Crazy? The only place things are what they should be is at five-star gourmet restaurants because dumbheads don't prepare $100 degustations.

We are interviewing Dr. Bernie M. in the New York City teaching hospital where he is head of oncology. He is a practitioner and researcher. A thin man of average height, Bernie is an articulate spokesman for patient's rights and high-quality medical care. He is all charged up. He leans forward when he speaks. He is intense, punctuating his key phrases with karate choplike arm movements. Names and places have been changed.

Generating Patients

Medicine today is a business. And the goal of the business, the reason somebody started the business in the first place, is to make a profit. The reason we have a healthcare structure is to care for people that are ill and to make people's health overall better. Granted, I think most people will accept the fact that we cannot do that in an economically irresponsible way. But still, the number one priority, the reason the healthcare endeavor is started, is to care for people's health.

The other thing to realize is that nobody started an HMO because they said, "Hmm, healthcare costs a lot and HMOs theoretically can deliver care for less and I want to be good to my society and deliver care for less." Nobody did that. Everyone looked at this and said, "You know, there's a lot of money changing hands in healthcare and I want some of it." So just as much money is paid out today as was ever paid out for healthcare. However, only 70 percent of that actually gets delivered to the healthcare organization. The other 30 percent is business expenses for the newly created middlemen.

I think what has happened is healthcare's been stood on its head. The goal of the healthcare industry is to make a profit now. And your product just happens to be caring for people. And whatever you can do, and get people to swallow, so that you can maximize your profit has to be okay.

You sit in some of these meetings and the terms that they use are purely business terms. They talk about "product lines." The first time I heard this I couldn't believe it. I felt like saying that we're not out there trying to convince people that they should have their arteries replaced or something like that. We're here if they need it. But we shouldn't be out there trying to get people to do more of this stuff if they don't need it.

Let's play on people's fear about cancer. Let's attract all the cancer patients we can attract. Let's make sure that we—here's the best example—let's make sure that we offer the kinds of cancer treatments that will draw people here. Not because it will be best for the people and not because it will optimize the chance of either curing their cancer or allowing them to live the longest and the best, but because it will bring the greatest number of patients here so that we will get the money.

Are physicians uncomfortable with that? Oftentimes, for instance if there's a consultant that comes in, a consultant will assume that they are preaching to the choir. I have had a couple of absolutely frightening experiences.

A Specialist for My Family

There was a consultant who came in. The guy was a physician, and he had gone to management school. He talked to the primary care physicians about managing the patients better so that inappropriate things are not done and so that more expensive drugs are not used and talked about it in terms of appropriate care for patients and appropriate quality.

And then when he met with the leadership group, who had more to do with the business aspect, one of the primary care physicians who was a member of both groups said, "Well, what about quality?" And the guy's attitude was absolutely different and he said, "Let's be honest. Nobody will ever be able to measure quality in our lifetime. So as long as we don't do anything that is just grossly wrong and stands out, we can do whatever we want."

We had a session about managed care. And there was some management executive person there talking about restricting access. And if you have somebody go to a specialist, it's more expensive.

And so somebody raised their hand and asked, "What happens if somebody in your family gets sick?" This guy was so disconnected from reality that he said, "Well, that doesn't matter to me. See, I'm so well connected I can get any member of my family to see any doctor anytime." And as far as he was concerned, that was an acceptable answer because he is so disconnected from what really happens. And people were astounded that this guy would say this in front of everybody, but that—he didn't realize what he was saying—but it reflected his reality.

People who start out in the management of a healthcare company think about the financial end of things. They spend most of their time trying to cut back on expenditures. Then they get a bad disease. I don't like to wish that on anybody, but someone gets breast cancer. Or prostate cancer or heart disease. If they're not one of the absolute top dogs, then all of sudden they are put in the same position as the people that they used to deny care to.

Quality Is a Paper Trail

A woman who runs a health plan in southern California came in. And she was talking about all the things to do to make it more profitable. And she was talking about how physicians only get 15 to 20 minutes with each patient no matter what. So somebody asked, "What about patients that are old and sick?" She says, "Tough, 15 to 20 minutes." If they have more than one problem, they have to make more than one appointment. That's just the way it is.

So people raised the question of quality. She said, "Oh, you have to realize that there is only one measure of quality today. That is life or death." If a person is alive, it's a success. And she's right. There is no other measure of quality today. So all that stuff you see in print and on television about high quality, etc., etc., is just public relations.

The vast majority of the certification things that hospitals go through is all a paper trail. Do you keep your records properly? And so they hire consultants to come in and do sort of a practice visit. I happened to be attending up on the floor. And all these suits [laughs] were in the conference room looking for the patient charts, which you're not supposed to do. So I went in and said, "Excuse me, can I help you?" They told me, "No, we're here just getting ready for the JACAHO visit." I said, "So what do you check?" "Well, we're checking for documentation." And up until this point, I thought they always checked quality. Stupid, right? I said, "Documentation? So you mean you're not checking to see how we do things." "No, we just want to know if it's documented." "You mean, you don't really care if I've gone out there and hacked up one of the patients with an ax?" The guy could see where I was going and he sort of laughed sheepishly. And he said, "You know, actually it's true. We don't care. All we care about is that you've documented it, so if you did hack up one of your patients and you documented it, we'd be happy. You would have fulfilled the criteria of the review."

So against that background, this consultant says you have to realize, and she's right, so she said, "Right now, there are only two measures of quality. One is life and one is death. So as long as someone draws a breath, they're counted as a success." She's right. And she said, "We are a health plan. We serve a million or 2 million people. Therefore, the only thing that will make us look bad is if the death rate changes in our population." She says, "If you deal with a big enough population, there are only two things that are going to change the death rate. One is a natural disaster, and if that happens, nobody will blame us. The other is an outbreak of infectious diseases. We immunize everybody for purely economic reasons." It also turns out that immunization is smart, but they're not doing it from a public health standpoint. In that case, actually, the economics causes good medical practice. I said, "So, what about patients who are old and sick and have a lot of problems?" She said, "They signed up for the healthcare plan, and if they don't like it, when it comes time for the open enrollment, they can go somewhere else. Otherwise, they have to go by our rules."

Somebody asked if they weren't unhappy. She said, "Of course they're unhappy. But if they're that sick, they're usually spending so much of their time and energy dealing with illness that they can't make life miserable for us. And frankly, it doesn't bother us that much." She said, "The vast majority of the population is either healthy or they have an illness that can be quickly dealt with," and she's right. And so the analogy that somebody drew and she agreed with is this: If you owned a grocery store and 95 percent of your customers were happy and brought you a profit and 5 percent of your customers were unhappy and cost you money, would you go out of your way to make those other 5 percent happy? No. You would hope that they went to some other grocery store. And that's exactly their point.

Actually, it is never transmitted in such bald terms to practicing physicians. That was the rationale. The way it's transmitted is financial exigencies are such that we absolutely must do it this way. Otherwise, we become uncompetitive, nobody will sign up with our health plan, we'll have no money coming in the door, and we'll all lose our jobs.

Parting Words

There was a fairly accomplished physician who was getting ready to retire. And we had a special dinner for him and he said, "No one is happier than me today." He said, "You know, you've always heard people talk about how pleased they are to retire and to get to do what they want to do. I share that, but I am especially happy because I'm getting out of medicine when it's turning into something I never wanted it to be."

He continued, "And I also find that a fair number of physicians who are probably in their mid-thirties and beyond are increasingly bitter because they get one message from their patients and their hearts and they get another message from the people who are really holding the pursestrings. One of the remarkable things that I have found—there have always been folks that have gone into medicine for the money—and they have been less affected by all of these changes because their target was money all along. So when the system changed, they said, 'Hold it, I've got to change the way I do things because I want to make money.' Whereas, the people who went into it for what most of us would consider to be the right reasons, have really been the ones that have been shackled by this."

MEANINGS AND LESSONS

This breathtaking ride through the healthcare field may be more than you or we wanted to know. The broad-ranging view reminds us of a gondola trip over the San Diego Wildlife Park where animals are observed from a safe distance. Bernie carries us aloft with clarifying descriptions offering an almost anthropological view. Riding comfortably on his words, you can pretend to be the observer in an unfamiliar landscape. That would be a mistake. Bernie is exposing the hypocrisy of healthcare leadership, the dehumanized public cant of concern, and the danger to the average consumer of services. You are a business.

He portrays a cultural upheaval between the new business medicine and the old patient medicine. New medicine wins. Healthcare facilities broker our health needs to captive hospitals and physicians. Thirty percent of the money collected goes to administrators for bringing doctor and patient together.

Bernie, too, is a captive of the system. Some physicians, greedy when they entered the field, are beating the drums and leading the parade toward personal wealth. Among the physicians, some of whom are wavering, he finds many torn between personal values and economic enticements. Mixed in on the sidelines are the happy older physicians, thankful they can get out with ethics intact.

The new definitions of quality—breathing or not breathing, just document what you do—may be alarming. Where is the notion of excellence? Go that route and you'll end up in a Honda or Toyota plant, not in a hospital. When you own the system, you can make up any regulations you want. Twisting words and creating rules to increase profitability have been raised to a high level in managed care. All done in the name of a free market.

LESSON

Stupid management is more noticeable—and more unforgivable—in the healthcare industry. When making a profit is the only measure of quality, people's lives are literally put in jeopardy.

Heartless, excessive constraints, help denied, long waits, 15 minutes a visit, you're too sick to fight us, go somewhere else, only healthy people wanted, you're going to die anyway, no specialists, that operation costs too much—what associations come to mind? We bet you don't think: Peace Corps, Mother Teresa, Albert Schweitzer, Martin Luther King, Jr., Gandhi, Jesus Christ.

We've attended meetings and panel discussions about managed care, read about the fraudulent behavior of leaders (Columbia/HMA, for example), and listened to many Bernies. We feel the shock. We hear about the political considerations, but why should we expect leaders in managed-care systems to have attitudes different from their counterparts in the rest of our market-driven economy?

LESSON

If dumbness in the handling of employees blankets the economy, why do we expect it to be different in handling patients?

Managed care—in other words, medicine—has finally become a true reflection of today's organizational values. How can we think it can really be fixed when we haven't yet fixed airline safety, when drug company researchers fabricate results, and when education isn't educating? What needs "fixing" are the values that permit all those atrocities to happen. Dumbness at the top!

BIKER CHICK

The name given to this story was hung on a director of nursing from hell by a nurse. Gruff, raw, loud, and dirty-mouthed, the biker chick ruled over the largest section of a religious retirement community where no one was supposed to curse. The story is told by Bev, a clinic nurse who was fired, and it describes a botched attempt to bring an old-line healthcare organization into a managed-care format. Bev and her husband came to our offices carrying a box of touching "goodbye" notes.

Bev's in her midfifties, spare and angular, and speaks in a high-pitched voice which occasionally approaches a screech. Her delivery is surprisingly detached considering the drama she's experienced. She seems washed out. Her husband, Jim, leans forward often as if to prompt her but restrains himself except for one point toward the end where he provides an economic analysis of managed care. Names and places have been changed.

I had been the nurse at a clinic at a retirement community for 2 years, and then Margaret, a new director of nursing, was hired. My first encounter with her was when I was called into her office and asked how I could let some resident come home from the hospital to her independent apartment. She was having no dementia problems, she knew her medication, and the doctor had discharged her from the hospital. I felt that my decision was just not that important in the whole of things. She came home, and instead of doing what she had been instructed to do, she laid around, and of course her pneumonia exacerbated, and she ended up being put back in the hospital.

This was a retirement community that had four different levels of care, and I was the clinic nurse in the independent living section. That was the highest level. Clinic nurse means nurse in charge. The census was between 350 and 400. Margaret was responsible for all four sections, which had close to 500 people.

Of course I was shocked. Yes, I really was. I wasn't expecting that kind of reaction from a director of nursing. Well, I was scheduled for a yearly review and was ripped from one end to the other. And at that point in time, I started to refute. I wrote back to the nurse and said I felt that it was totally unfair, how I felt about the review, and what should have been said. The correspondence continued for a year. Oh, I also was denied a raise at that time.

The next review after that was better, and I was allowed to have a raise, but all the time we continued to correspond back and forth over these allegations they were making about my capabilities, my character, and my feelings, which had never been discussed with them, so they didn't know how I felt about things anyway.

They gave lip service to being a team, but in reality they wanted people to agree with them and say "yes" and not do any thinking on their own. It was a power administration with verbal lip service to teams.

Once a week we would have a resident care conference and the administrator of the healthcare was the chairman of the healthcare conference, and if I heard him say it once, I heard him say it I don't know how many times that we are a team and everybody counts as an individual on the team. But when push came to shove, that is not what he meant. He meant, "I'm in charge, I have the power, and you agree or you will have problems."

No, I can't explain why. I don't know. Whether he was insecure, afraid to let other people make decisions, or wanting complete power over other people. I think all are possibilities. The person with the greatest status in terms of training would have been Margaret and then came me.

Then they started write-ups. And anytime that I did something they perceived was wrong, I got a derogatory write-up from the director of nursing. And some of these things that I was accused of were taken right from their own policies. She was someone whose word was law, and it didn't make any difference whether it was right or wrong. It was her word, and the way she wants it is the way it's going to be.

She was not very loving. She could, in my opinion, be very-two faced. She would put on a very concerned act when families of residents were around and act exactly the opposite when no family was around. The administrator was like that, too. I understand that the two of them got into screaming and shouting matches a lot over at healthcare, and some rather nasty words were exchanged. You have to understand that this was a religious organization, and so swearing and using words that were off-color were really not allowed.

So finally I was fired. They tried to make me resign. They informed me that I was relieved of my duties as clinic nurse. And I had a choice of becoming a staff nurse at [another facility] on P.M.s or nights or a night supervisor. And if I was not willing to take either one of those two positions, then they would consider that I had turned in my resignation. I was unwilling to take either of their offers, and so my position is that I was fired. And so I subsequently applied for unemployment insurance, which the organization fought, but the final judgment by the unemployment association was that yes, indeed, I was fired and I was entitled to the unemployment benefits. They supported me in my statement that I was fired.

The real reason I was fired was because the administration couldn't trust me to be a "yes" person.

Jim's Analysis

I think she was fired because she ended up having an unbelievable relationship with as many of those 400 people as you can. She still gets cards from them. And that was the real intent in independent living...to have a relationship with those people, to urge them on to be independent, to analyze them, and to move them on to this next area of care. She knew that a lot of these people came in, gave them all their money, and the institution said we will take care of you. Well, they were playing games with that. They were playing games with kicking people out of the hospital early so that they would have to go to some outside service and pay for it themselves. They were playing games with doing the opposite where they had to move somebody from one care to the other care so they could get more money from the state. Or they had beds fill up in the higher income thing.

Bev was trying to play by the rules. And these other people were playing by some hidden agenda which not necessarily everybody knew. There was fear of her logic and her liking by the patients and her ability to cut through and get to the heart of the matter where they had all these peripheral things going on. They moved one woman from independent care to another level because she was having trouble pulling up her pants. What they got was a very nice apartment to resell. And most of the residents considered if they left independent and went to [another facility], they went there to die. You were going to die soon. If you have a skilled care facility here, the idea is to keep those beds as full as you can all the time. She was the one who had to go to say to the family, "We're now taking your aunt, who you're paying for, and we're going to move her." The resident care committee made those decisions.

Bev's Conclusion

I agree with Jim's analysis. Basically I considered myself a resident advocate and I don't know if they wanted a resident advocate in that position. A nurse called Margaret, a biker chick. She was hard and loud.

MEANINGS AND LESSONS

This story could have been called "Nurse Cares Meets Nurse Doesn't Care." As Bev explains, her organization nationwide has always had a superb reputation. In her facility, "new" kinds of people were brought in to confront the challenge of maximizing profits for the whole system. It was achieved two ways: (1) manipulating and upgrading categories of care—that's already been documented in Medicare and Medicaid exposés—so as to increase revenues and (2) destroying values that placed people above dollars, the kind transmitted to the residents by nurses like Bev.

There are two interlocking themes. One is how the dumb boss, Margaret, sets out to get rid of a popular clinic nurse. The other is how caring, compassion, and playing by the rules confound a healthcare system determined to increase profits.

Dedicated nurses define "dumb" as less patient care. Managed-care administrators define "dumb" as decreased profit.

LESSON

When profits are concerned, bad nursing—doing more by giving less—wins out over good nursing—doing more by giving more.

Bev didn't know what hit her. Her husband spotted it immediately and pushed her into action. What hit her was a culture-driven slap in the face delivered by a brash nurse. It took 2 years for the system to purge her. She had the residents on her side while the administration was busy establishing their brand of unfeeling leadership throughout the facility.

The personality conflict between Bev and Margaret runs deep. Implied, but not openly stated, in her story was the difference in economic level and lifestyle—comfortable Bev versus struggling Margaret. Then there was the coterie of residents waving "We Want Bev" flags, a real put-down to Margaret. A reading of letters she received portrays her floating along on a group-generated cloud of good feeling. Observing that call to arms for a popular nurse must have driven a woman like Margaret senseless. Urged on by Jim, Bev became counteraggressive. She endured harassment and kept taking it—those notorious write-ups—but ultimately caved in and left.

LESSON

If you choose to take up arms against your employer, it helps to have a spouse or significant other who can support you.

But we're losing track of the residents. There are incidents similar to this across the country that place patients at the bottom. People are mentioned last in their role as human beings in need of help, the element to which naive Bev was responding.

INSANITY

Decisions of no decision are one way to manage a multinational corporation under siege. That is not as easy as it may sound. It's actually brilliant. What it entails is a group of well-paid, high-status executives doing dumb while appearing smart. This big-picture story is told by Dan, a smart administrative manager. He's an incisive analyst and knows contradiction when he sees it. His heart is breaking, his eyes look sad, and that's not comfortable to watch in a large man who's obviously had a successful career. Dan has been with the corporation for more than 20 years and remembers when they had an unbeatable reputation for quality. Now things are different. We're talking with him in our offices. Names and places have been changed.

> We get together in the business meetings and talk about a lot of things. We rarely make any decisions. And my job is to facilitate a lot of those kinds of meetings. The management shies away from making tough decisions, especially around anything that is not a financial area. Financials they can make decisions about because they can see the numbers and say, "Oh my God, they're going south. We gotta' do something." So they knee jerk and do something and they try to make the numbers go north.
>
> But the thing that I observe most is when they don't make a decision; they don't realize that no decision is a decision. A lack of a decision is a decision.
>
> Then they moan and groan about spending too much time in meetings. The fact is they are very ineffective in their own decision-making process. And for a quality corporation, that is just a big, big red flag.
>
> A quality corporation is one that has the reputation for building and delivering quality products and services to the consuming public. Those attributes were true in the past. Now the one thing this corporation is very good at is restructuring—the classic corporate America tool to success.

You draw boxes on an old chart and put new names in the boxes and add new titles. But what really has to happen for it to make sense to the stakeholders and the corporation is that somehow we have to redefine products and services. The work that is done to make those products and services has to add value for the consuming public. We don't do that. It's done all the time in corporate America, and our company is no different than any other company in the sense that we restructure every time the stock market analysts say you're a so-so performer. So you get a little bit of a bump in the stock market because you did restructuring. And you claim all kinds of savings. Most of the savings come from reduced payroll.

Basically, when you restructure, you eliminate certain numbers of bodies and you retitle people. But if you haven't redefined the work and reskilled people to do the job—their new job in the new environment—what does that person do? They do what they know best. They try to do the new job the way they've done the old job. It's the classic definition of insanity—doing the same old thing the same way and expecting different results.

Here's the way it was put by one consultant to our management. The consultant said, "You know, every time a part of your organization gets into financial trouble, you restructure it. Question: Has it ever done any good?" No answer.

Look, we're a midwestern corporation. What's missing is a sense of entrepreneurship, somebody who can take a look at the big picture in the marketplace and decide on an action and move it forward. We're a midwestern company with midwestern business values. We have a history of hiring midwestern trained and bred technical employees, emphasis on the word technical. Those kinds of people are promoted and moved through the corporation because of their technical expertise and their ability to develop and deliver on technical stuff, hardware. They are promoted for their success in technical areas. So, the senior-level people in the corporation are technocrats. They are not truly entrepreneurs in a business sense.

Our industry's business environment is changing radically. We have a lot of technical managers who are risk averse, and they're not very good strategists. So what happens is they try to do more of the same, faster, harder, longer, and it just isn't getting us anywhere. Instead of looking at that critical asset that will make us different from everybody else, i.e., people, they're looking at financials, hardware, technology, and restructuring. They think all we have to do is move people around and put them in different jobs and it will happen.

What we should do is accomplish what it takes to have people do their jobs better, faster, and more productively than the same people amongst our competitors. This leads to frustration. There's very little learning going on. If you're in the middle of the pack—like us—that's mediocrity. If you're leading the pack, "I'm the leader," but if the whole pack is mediocre in its performance in that spectrum of the world market, it's still mediocrity. And that's where we're at. We delight in mediocrity.

MEANINGS AND LESSONS

Dan is eloquent in his analysis and may be on the verge of dreaming the wild dreams needed to help his company. He can't quite grab those dreams. His own history stops him: He's still loyal to the meaning of his job and does his job, but does he have the power or the allies to change things? His is a remarkable statement of how original smart evolves first into dumb and then into truly dumb. But what special technology does Dan have to move his company into a different way of doing business with its customers and employees? He has none.

It's as if he would wish to take a massive structure like Chicago's Union Station—in keeping with the midwestern locale—back to a time when the mighty 20th Century Limited barrelled into town rather than Amtrak, its weak offspring. Then the technology fit the setting. But now the technology is wrong for today's business environment.

LESSON
Restructuring is like a home built on terraced foothills near Los Angeles. A big storm can wash everything away.

Can Dan's story be generalized? He's talking about much more than an authoritative versus participative style of management. The true meaning is to be found in his description of the meetings he facilitates, in what senior managers can and cannot accept as what should be included in the definition of reality. Dan ticks them off for us: accepted are finance, engineering, process, technology, hardware; rejected are people and their training.

His questions are potent ones. How can technocrats handle people in more constructive ways? How can technocrats be made to see that doing the "same old, same old" and more of it is not a solution to anything? How do technocrats renounce the knee-jerk form of restructuring? How do technocrats turn themselves inside out? The answers are they can't, they won't, they don't care to, and why should they?

Dan is stuck, knows it, and is unhappy. Many in his organization are similarly stuck and may know it at varying levels of consciousness but cannot afford to be unhappy. They have jobs, but unlike Dan, they may not be thinkers and poets. His senior managers have little to fear. Some day, someone will come along and tear down the Union Station, but by then Dan's antagonists will have retired to warmer climates. In those places, in gated golf course communities, they will probably run into other technocrats enjoying themselves. Dan? We hope he writes his memoirs because he sure does have a great vantage point from which to do so.

LESSON

In a truly dumb organization, you must keep thinking, talking, reading, and writing. One day you might be needed.

I WORKED FOR A GENIUS

The genius leader described here is someone to be avoided. Our informant, Pete, will explain why and escort you into a prototype dysfunctional (his word) culture. To be known as "the resident genius," said with eyes rolling, is the ultimate put-down. After all, the guy you're about to meet was the executive vice president and he had power. He was pathetic, a failed genius who played with the humanity of hundreds.

We met with Pete in a relatively quiet spot at an electronics trade show. He is the friend of a friend and agreed to tell us about his experiences with a former employer. Pete's a thoughtful, straight-talking man in his early fifties, balding, a little overweight, unkempt looking from having struggled through vast exhibit halls. He gets to the point quickly. Names and places have been changed.

ElectroX is about a $50 million company and I was there for 15 years. I originally came in as customer service manager and became copy chief. At the time, the company was under the direction of a close friend of the founder. He retired and the son took over the company. The son had an engineering background. All of a sudden, engineering became a very important part of the company as opposed to marketing, which was the ex-vice president's background. And then everyone reported to the new vice president, Rich Reaser. Even if you didn't report to him, he treated you as if you reported to him.

The owner and Rich huddled together all the time. No one knew what was going on. They'd call people in, and when they came out, they looked ashen. Then you'd hear loud laughter. People were seldom fired.

Rich controlled everything. It was run under a direction of fear. Everybody in the company was afraid of this one vice president. He wielded so much power. And he was a very unstable person. He was a very emotional person. Other than having a very unhappy home life, he had a very poor self-image. He was an engineer and close personal friend of the president. He was a very bright man. And I think he was probably too bright for the company. He should probably have been sequestered somewhere in a closet and just let him work on a project.

He had no human relations skills, no people skills, no management skills. I think the most disturbing thing to me is that he felt that by reading a book he could accomplish any task better than any person who worked for the company. He felt that by reading a book on marketing, my field, he could become a marketer.

He forgot all the emotional aspects of the job. He would second-guess everybody. One time he came to my office screaming and hollering and using every four-letter word in the book about copy that we had written. No sooner had he walked out than all the writers came out of their offices with clips from newspapers and magazines showing that the grammar usage that one of the writers had used was correct. Rich just didn't understand that things had changed. He said, "Nobody writes like that, nobody. It's the dumbest thing in the world." He said something to the effect that, "If you prove me wrong, I'll take you out for a steak dinner." Later, I showed him all the clips that the other writers brought out, but he never apologized. And I never got the steak dinner.

Rich knew everything about everything and he had developed a model for the analysis of media. And for half an hour, he went through this whole thing. He acted as though he was so smart and I was just fortunate to be sitting at his feet. At the end of his half-hour lecture, he said "Do you understand what I just showed you?" I said, "Pretty much, but I really don't have to because I got the same answer you did." He did not like that answer at all.

We had confrontations all the time, and I think he respected the fact that I offered an opposing opinion. If you don't wimp out, you get further. Few people were ever fired; they stayed out of his way. Very often he would talk to me about personal problems. I would give him my opinions on it, and he seemed to respect my opinion.

I think I know why he behaved like he did at work; he was not a good-looking man. He was aging and he was going through almost like a midlife crisis. Here he was, supposedly as smart as he was. When I first came to the company, somebody told me about the resident genius. He was the resident genius. And I don't think he had a lot of success in his life, in the company, and in his personal life. He had so much anger and suspicion built up in him that it's hard to imagine somebody would have a home life with that much anger and suspicion. And I think the president furthered this. He gave engineering the power, and since he controlled this person, it gave the president more power. It became an engineering-run company, not a marketing-driven company, and they lost tremendous market share. Because the other companies had people in marketing who grew up in marketing, but didn't need to read the book. They experienced it. They lost sales and lost the loyalty of their distributors. They fell behind in product innovation only because one person controlled everything.

It's funny. It was a privately owned corporation, and every penny you spent is the owner's money. Therefore, if the owner doesn't see the value in it, money isn't spent, even though it should have been spent. I remember during the energy crisis they turned off the power and turned down the lights and after the crisis the lights didn't go back on. They saved money and that money went into the president's pocket. Rich was not putting money into his pocket.

Quality wasn't lost; they had pride of engineering. But they lost in innovation. It wasn't a healthy environment. I think of all the people who were dressed-down in public. They ran the organization by fear rather than by management. Based on that, I've said I will never work for a privately owned organization again. I had a boss who had a heart attack. He was constantly berated by Rich, who always knew better than everybody else. Rich was the laughing stock of the company. You know, when you have fear, people talk behind your back.

The lessons I learned? When you see that environment coming, get out. I guess it's like getting divorced; you always look for some positive aspect of the relationship because you have that hope. I could live with it. I was not happy with it, but there weren't any jobs out there that I wanted to do. I would come home every night and my wife would say, "Stop complaining already, stop complaining already. You have a lot of friends there; you have a certain comfort level with the company." It was convenient to my house. I had a lot of people who relied on me and I treated them fairly. I could protect my people from Rich. My boss did the same for me, but he wasn't too strong or as bright as he should have been.

Rich retired, but my informants tell me it's not any better. The seeds are planted. The family is still involved in the business. Rich was protecting the owner's pennies. And they're still concerned with the pennies. The culture is run on fear. After I left I said that if they would call me back and quadruple my salary, I wouldn't go back. It wasn't a healthy environment. It didn't foster creativity; it didn't make you want to go to work each day. It wasn't a fun place to work. You're there 8 hours a day. It was completely dysfunctional.

MEANINGS AND LESSONS

This is an instance of "wild leadership" (from the concept "wild analysis," which describes the perversion of psychotherapy in the hands of an irresponsible practitioner) embedded within a disturbed organization. To be given the dictatorial powers Pete describes, Rich had to be a co-conspirator, a toady off stage and a martinet on stage. The conspiracy was about maintaining a sickness in the way the company was run, where decisions were made behind closed doors for every department.

Pete talks about management by fear. He doesn't mean fear of job loss. Pete was able to protect his people. The engineers were safe. It wasn't dollars and cents fear. It was fear of the bully who in this case, in addition to being mean, suspicious, and egomaniacal, was also bright.

Pete says the whole environment was dysfunctional and infers it is traceable to Rich's emotional problems. It's a plausible explanation but misses a significant element. Recall, Pete takes Rich's torments for almost 15 years. That sounds like more torture than anyone should be expected to endure. And he is not alone in adapting to the wild man's style. Others, too, stayed and took it.

LESSON

Adapting to a wild leader in a crazy culture is like being the fox in a blood-sport hunt. You may be quick, clever, and nimble, but you'll still be killed at the end of the game.

When Pete leaves, he discovers the culture doesn't change, explaining "the seeds were planted," but the more relevant explanation can be found in his remarking that the company is pinching pennies and the family is still there. The president is the true source of organizational dysfunction. No one stops him, and therefore, no one could stop Rich.

LESSON

The toady subleader absorbs that green, gooey stuff produced by the top alien and becomes even uglier than the host.

HELLO CORPORATE CULTURE, GOOD-BYE

Anything we want can be had for a price. It's the basis of the world's economies, so why not a corporate culture? The idea of buying a corporate culture is not crazy. CEOs who mingle among those who have been rewarded with cabinet posts and ambassadorships find nothing strange in assuming that a corporate culture can be bought. All you need is the "fixer" who can get the money to the right place. That's exactly what Vic and Joyce thought—throw dollars at it. Their story was reported in *The Wall Street Journal.* To make sense of it, we had to read the article standing on our heads.

I WANT THAT!

The Wall Street Journal, April 11, 1997
Atlanta

Their eyes sparkled with enthusiasm—10 young, fresh-faced graduates, all smiling broadly on the cover of *Fortune* in May 1994. They worked for Architectural Support Services, Inc., or ASSI, "a company," the magazine cover declared, "where employees take charge of their futures."

And how. Within a year, all but two of them had walked out, embittered and divided against the very company that gave them control. . . . What on earth went wrong? Though their concepts were sound, the owners' execution was flawed . . .

Vic and Joyce (owners and married business partners) followed a rigorous recruiting profile, hiring hotshot young designers from the best schools. They built a look-alike staff of people between 21 and 23 years old, most from well-to-do backgrounds. Though gifted at organizing, Joyce was uneasy about her people skills. She immersed herself in books, tapes and seminars that appealed to her sensibilities as a rebellious baby boomer. Teams. Empowerment. Profit sharing. No hierarchies. It was her extensive use of these policies that put her and her employees on the cover of *Fortune. Later the company was featured in a management textbook as a case study in modern management* (emphasis ours).

But while experts were fawning, the staff was fuming. Employees were expected to schedule their own jobs, but they were offended if Vic pointed out they were behind schedule. They were asked to deal directly with customers, but they chafed when customers made big demands. When the owners leased an extra-large suite so everyone could sit by a window, employees complained about the glare on their computer screens. When Joyce offered to send people to professional development classes, they took it as a slight.

The reality, in retrospect, wasn't terribly complicated. Joyce and Vic had given their young staff plenty of authority but too little accountability. There were no performance reviews. No one was ever fired. They had created not a sense of fulfillment, but of entitlement . . . So finally, early in 1995, the "walkout" began. In the space of a few weeks the entire design staff (but one) jumped to clients and competitors.

MEANINGS AND LESSONS

There is a miniature example of a rush toward a management mirage and promise of greatness. As heat waves alter perception, management theorists have clouded the vision of organizations starved for easily grasped solutions to massive changes in the workplace. But let's be fair to Joyce and Vic, because for intent, motivation, homework, decency, and compassion they deserve A's. The article gives them an F for poor execution. Missed was the gullibility category for which Joyce and Vic earn another A.

The gullibility factor links all frightened organizations together. Desperate for a fast route to success, and conditioned to believe celebrity business authors, corporations do pratfalls over gurus who promote what become, in retrospect, dumb fads.

LESSON

A dumb fad is an idea embraced by gullible organizations who don't know you can't imitate another company's culture.

Are you thinking, what's wrong with empowerment, flat hierarchies, and teams? It's this: They don't quite mesh with the human animal in business, something most organizations learn once they set aside their impossible dreams and confront the real world of work. Those uplifting ideas are philosophical carrots and don't help employees win the competitive race at work. Sure, we love apple pie and I, too, want to be in *Fortune* anyway I can.

Leaders feel ennobled when they proclaim their employees are empowered and make speeches about a climate of cooperation. Then? Dead quiet. Where's the heaven on earth that was supposed to result? Why are people so ungrateful? If nothing else, corporate leaders can face their makers with clear consciences.

HANDLING MILLIONS WHILE ON FOOD STAMPS

A secretary's tale. Mary moved to Arizona, took a job at a bank—didn't need the money but wanted to work—and forced her boss president to treat her decently. She had nothing to lose. Her story is about how a demotivating culture is born. She recalls an event that took place 10 years earlier. We report it because it is still taking place.

We're sitting at her kitchen table, drinking coffee. Mary spends a great deal of time putting on her makeup and selecting her clothes—she has always been that way—although she seldom leaves the house. A tall woman, a real pusher of a person, she had married a sweet, quiet, and very considerate man. Then he was gone. She's thankful for our visit. Names and places have been changed.

He was a CEO at this bank, very intelligent. I moved here from Chicago after my husband died suddenly and started working at two-thirds of what I used to make. Arizona does not pay very well. When I was hired, they promised me a 10 percent raise within 90 days. But when the time came, my boss said, "I really can't authorize this raise."

Like the government, everybody had a grade and I was already beyond what my grade called for. He ran the whole place, so I said to him, "You can do anything; make my grade higher." "I'd really like to," he said, "but you know we can't do it for one. We have 500 employees. We'd have to do it for everybody."

"I've got faith in you," I told him. "You promised. I know you'll get it. You know, I spend more money in a week than you pay me for a month [laughs and laughs]. It isn't that I need it, but you promised me and I want it." And I got it! [exulted]

They were so cheap. What bothered me the most—it made me sick and still does to think about it—was our bank tellers. They were mostly single mothers working. All on food stamps. That's how little money they made.

And you know the fellows that ran it, that started the bank, were all millionaires, and their bonuses were so much, and here these poor tellers needed food stamps to survive.

I used to tell him about that. What did I have to lose? I'd say, "Aren't you ashamed to work at a place where your employees are on food stamps?" He said, "That's how I started, too. That's what you have to do when you're in the banking business. Start out low."

MEANINGS AND LESSONS

Mary's is not a sweeping story. It doesn't arouse strong passions. She does, however, explain a survival technique that can work under certain circumstances.

═══════════════════════════════════════

LESSON

Don't play "chicken" with your boss, because if you go off the road, you better land in a pile of money.

═══════════════════════════════════════

From such small events, repeated again and again throughout all industries, two opposed pictures of the workplace emerge. One is illusory: "We're wonderful; we're visionaries who revel in chaos." It's a world that exists in the minds of some millennium and futurist experts, and sometimes it can look and sound like a cult.

LESSON

If the economy makes a huge dip down and a visionary emerges to suggest, "Let's all jump into the drink and enter organizational heaven together," don't do it.

Then there is the real world, Mary's, with which most people contend. In that world, loyalty is reserved for one's family and a culture is defined by uncomplicated, direct, and easily understood events. Mary had enough resources to defy her shortsighted, thickheaded boss and got away with it. The reasons most employees would never dream of using Mary's ploy can be understood on three counts. The rationale: Use prudence in avoiding too risky a gamble. The odds are better in the gaming industry where upwards of 90 percent of all money wagered is returned to the players. The psychological: Aggression toward a boss—even a thickheaded one—will arouse fear of rejection. The spiritual: Don't tamper with the harmony of nature.

CHURCH AND BUSINESS DON'T MIX

Church is supposed to bond people together. Right? It didn't do it for Maysie in New Orleans. She's a self-employed mortgage broker, well-groomed, pink, and plumpish, in her early forties. It's late afternoon and the sun is streaming in through the blinds. She's telling us about a rigidly pompous ass who took title to mean ascendancy.

Maysie works hard and is successful. She's happy, generous, and smiles and laughs a lot. Her face looks like those happy face images people append to notes. Even though her event occurred years ago, she still has trouble figuring it out. Why was he like that? She speaks in a high, sing-song voice, suddenly stops, looks at us intently, and then goes on. Names and places have been changed.

> My first job. For I can't remember how many years, Jack O. sat across the table from me at church. We went to church together for years, Sunday school, every Sunday. I go to work for First Money and the man never spoke to me again until I left. Why? I think it was dumb. [very excited] I mean, I know him personally. And my kids went to school with his kids, so why would me working at his bank, why all of a sudden—have I got poison ivy or something? He never said good morning. If you walked down the aisle, he'd turn his head. I thought it was because he's thinking, "I'm a big wheel; you're a nothing." Now if a big wheel talks to nothings, that might bring him down. It had to be something like that. If it were only in the bank, maybe I could understand, but I doubt it—I'm a big body; you're a nobody. But the church thing. He never sat by us again.
>
> It wasn't smart. You're only as good as your employees are. You don't shine unless they shine. And by putting down your employees, number one, you're causing bad feelings, and number two, fortunately he wasn't my immediate boss, but if he had been, do you think I would have really wanted to work hard for him?
>
> The whole bank was like that. Yes, he set the standard. If you were a male, you got promotions, you got this, you got that. If you were female, they were very chauvinistic. The other thing at First Money was that you did your job in this little spot, and what the person in the next desk did was none of your business. And that's a poor way to run a business because the more you know about the total picture, the better understanding you have about your job. So by limiting your scope, they're taking away from what you could perform. They had a big turnover of people. And they had the attitude that we'll hire somebody else for minimum wage.

MEANINGS AND LESSONS

A seemingly uncomplicated, no-big-deal story told by an engaging woman who documents another foolproof method for alienating employees. It's an important story because when a supervisor rejects an employee, it's inexcusably dumb. In Maysie's story, the fact that rejection occurred between people who used to commune in church says something about the way her boss interpreted the culture of the bank. He must have known that his snobbishness would be supported. What he didn't know was it could also be communicated to customers.

LESSON

When a manager you thought was a friend becomes a cold, pompous, unfeeling fish, it's in the culture, so watch out.

A question: Is there something about the culture of the finance industry that cultivates stupidity? This story is one of a number about that industry. What propels nonfeeling, nonempathic people to the top? Are they losers with no charm or winners with no charm? There is notorious Charles Keating of savings and loan fame as well as a few of President Clinton's Arkansas banking buddies—all personable and charming, some already in jail, and others perhaps destined for the same fate. Then there are the Swiss bankers, once paradigms of objective neutrality, discredited with a version of small town greed, sitting for decades on money entrusted to them during World War II.

It may be that when you manage a small bank, you can be a small jerk. But as you step up the ladder to where business and politics begin to mix, you must transform yourself with charm and con into a big jerk.

LESSON

Ode to Keating: "Oh what a shame for bankers with smarts for the world to discover they've been nothing but tarts."

We find jerks and charmers everywhere. Notice that jerks and charmers can be dumb, reduce efficiency and quality, and provoke turnover. Is it possible, you may ask, for a dumb leader to be smart in certain other ways and produce a sought-after product and make a profit?

Our stories explore that question. People tell of finding themselves part of systems so stupidly managed that no procedure could ever make it right. Amazingly, you'll discover how hard it is for employees to sever emotional ties to their employers, no matter how negative the experiences.

LESSON

Loyalty to one's employer is a difficult habit to kick. For some, it's tied to patriotism. Love your country, love your company used to be a strong family value.

Marketing types push the connection between corporate loyalty and national patriotism. But it's becoming a more difficult sell. When people recognize that country and company are indeed different, it's a maturing insight. It hasn't come unaided. When employees observe long-range smart being traded for short-range dumb, they become nervous about their jobs. Loyalty is being sacrificed for good-looking monthly and quarterly earnings reports, changing the culture of corporate life. Now it's every man and woman for themselves.

IF YOU GET SICK, YOU'RE FIRED

The culture killer in this story is a self-righteous, stubborn man, a trained accountant, whose near felonious behavior wrecked his company. Drew, the storyteller, is a CPA. When he left the company, he was their financial VP. He describes a boss positioning himself in a fortress on the top of a hill. No matter what assault weapons his managers used, they couldn't clamber over his walls. Many were wiped out. Drew's story is a combat report. Managers fought. The boss withstood their pressures. The organization withered inside. Sales of $35 million and 800 employees went down to $12 million and 100 employees. Those who got tired of fighting started rival operations which prospered.

Drew is now self-employed and says he couldn't be happier. He's a slight man, graying and somewhat hyper, all qualities which have proven to be positive for his new business. He stops as he makes a key point, stares at you, face turning red, and moves closer to get your undivided attention. Names and places have been changed.

The setting was we were looking for new business opportunities for a direct mail organization. An idea came to one of the people in marketing. The owner, the leader, was asking us to get more information. There was an element of risk. Ordinarily, you expect some risk in a new venture; it can't be eliminated. You can never have enough information. This marketing manager was fired just before the end of the fiscal year so he wouldn't have to be paid a bonus. So he went over and gave the idea to the competitor, which is now a $50 million business in the space of 6 years' time.

He's fired people left and right and they've gone to compete against him in the same product lines. His business is about 40 percent of what it was 6 years ago and falling like a rock. He felt employee turnover was a good thing. He honest to God thought that employee turnover was a good thing.

Incidents? This fellow—I think he was a maintenance man—the president asked him to do something in the building. But the man wasn't quite prepared and fell off a ladder and injured himself. The owner said, "Fire him." "What? Fire him? Why do you want to fire him?" He said, "We don't want to pay him while he's off."

I said it wasn't a wise business decision. I couldn't approach him on an ethical basis; it had to be dollars and cents. I told him, "You're risking our unemployment compensation. We'll get hit with it. He'll come back and he'll probably win." Which is what happened. It cost him $35,000, but then we were put into a risk pool, and the total insurance was two to three times more over a period.

He always felt that he could buy somebody in a lower salary level. Say he had a sales manager paying him $60,000 or $80,000, he gets somebody else new, comes in at $40,000, gives him raises to go up to $50,000 [face gets red and stares]—he feels he's saved all that money. Gets all the new ideas from him and then kinda lets him go. The other thing he felt, you know, FICA. He was a nitpicker, so if you keep it around $40,000 or $50,000, he saves money as well as profit sharing; they don't become vested.

Nothing was written. He would make promises, say we can do this, do that, you can have this. And when you got there, it never came to pass. After a year or two, he would start getting negative, which would be your first step on the way out the door.

And part of that, really Bill, is this mind-set with advice from the legal profession. "Don't reinforce the positive. You reinforce the negative. You say too many nice things about them, they can come back with some legal action saying you canned them because of age discrimination, sex discrimination," whatever you will. So in the personnel files, you have all negative things and you know he puts those in writing, with no basis in fact or a reply back from employees. Attorneys would say, "When you give a review, give a poor review."

When I started, the sales volume was only 2 or 3 million and they employed maybe 45 people. When I left, 35 million, two divisions, and close to around 800 people. Now the sales volume is down to about 12 million, and I think they have a total of 100 or so people. He's had two different series of managements in the last 6 years, none lasting more than 2 to 3 years. Each time they go through another shakedown, the sales have gone down. Many have little experience, so he's got real problems.

Why he did those things? Well, you know, he liked to see things in black and white. His background was an accountant and I was an accountant. He felt himself to be a marketing man and a leader. He was out of Arthur Andersen. "I gotcha!" was the attitude. Not how can I help you, but here's what you did, "I gotcha!"

When you're going into a leadership role, into management, running a company, and wanting to direct it, that attitude has to shift. You want to welcome new ideas if you want to grow a company, and if you want a revenue stream, you have to attract good people. His leadership wasn't leadership; it was negative reinforcement. He could never be persuaded to see any way but his.

He did things that were rather tactless. He would say things to people that would get them in tears. I mean literally. He would bypass the lines of authority and go right down, and here's this clerk getting bawled out by the president of the company. I mean, my God, she's in tears. Hovering and nitpicking!

Here he is looking at accounts payable. Hell, the damn business, let's get some other new lines. He's crossing the t's and dotting the i's, and the big picture has gone away. He looked at things and wanted to see short-term gain, like in employee turnover. Instead he got long-term pain. The company and him have suffered.

In a way, I enjoyed working there. I gained and learned a lot about growth, to see strategy. That part was fun. I just talked to another guy who was laid off and has gone on to another company. He's done much better. I loved the strategy part. I did love that. I had some of the best times.

MEANINGS AND LESSONS

Yes, dumb guys do run businesses for a while. And smart people work for them. The dumb guy receives no loyalty or trust. Dumb guys don't know how to care about others. Notice what happens to Drew and other managers who leave the company. And notice what happens to the owner.

LESSON

Dumb leaders get dumber while the smart people around them get smarter.

There is a silver lining. Drew knows he learned a lot. He studied stupidity up close. He applied what he learned to his own business, where he's a huge success.

LESSON

What all smart new graduates should pray for is that their first job be with a dumb leader who has created a miserable culture. That's how you learn.

Some still think you become smart in school, go out in the real world, and get rewarded. Not so. School is where you prove you are a learner. But you become smart studying dumb cultures on the job, up close and personally. Ask any consultant who's willing to be honest.

How long do you stay in that environment? Everything

else being equal, long enough to protect the credibility of your résumé and grasp the reasons why the organization has had its run.

When you observe an unresolvable struggle between smart managers and a rocklike, dumb boss, the time has come to leave.

We can't leave this without mentioning the alleged legal advice Drew's boss received about powerful management tools: the performance review and personnel folder. The attorney's recommendation to record only negative information in order to avoid lawsuits could be a complete fabrication, but it fits the emerging personality. Drew's boss and the attorney could represent a marriage made in heaven. Larcenous temperaments seeking like. Whatever the true facts, the scheme is reprehensible.

LESSON
When dumbness at the top insists on perpetuating itself, a miserable life for everyone else is assured.

EVERYTHING BECAME DUMBER

Starting out dumb is not unusual and can be forgiven because there's always the opportunity to learn as you grow. Jack, our storyteller, shows you a different version: a 30-year story ending up as a VP in "corporate."

This story demonstrates the difference between what can be called "big dumb culture" (this story) and "little dumb culture" (the story that follows). Big dumb grew internally and through acquisitions from about 175 million annually to about 300 million in spite of itself. Employment ranged from 1200 to 1500 people. Jack was a friend of a client and sat on this story like a memory that wouldn't go away. But once he started talking, he kept going and going.

If ever a man looked like Mr. Corporate America, it was Jack. Tall, gray, regular features, he would look equally good playing golf, in a board room, or mingling with workers on a plant floor. He is a charmingly self-deprecating, humorous man who spins a good tale. Raised in the rural midwest, he is a devoted son who finds time to visit his "ma," cuts her firewood, repairs her roof, and feels deeply when she gets sick. We're in his office in his new company, which he founded with a friend. It's everything he ever wanted, and at age 60, he's a happy man. Names and places have been changed.

Perhaps the best way is to start before my promotion into corporate. I'd been with the company for 25 years prior to my elevation to the rarified atmosphere. Started on the sales desk of a small company. I kept getting promoted. By this time, the company had merged with a larger company, and we became big enough to have a corporate group. At this stage, the happenings accelerated. A coup took place. The old chairman was deposed and a younger hotshot brought in from the east coast. Soon my company had a wheeler-dealer as its president.

The hotshot brought in several more east coast jerks to show 'em how the big boys did it. I was promoted to general manager of a small satellite plant and product line. It was underperforming their expectations. Being general manager of a small operation was a delight. You were far enough away from both company and corporate officers that you could get something done without having to check each detail with them. Like every plant I've been in, it had a core of good solid people that were really trying.

Even though we couldn't get much money for new equipment—I believe they were using us as a cash cow—we did a lot of innovative things with old discards from other plants. With a good team effort, lots of work, lots of fun, we started making great—well, good—profits. These were quickly devoured by the parent for building their superstar division.

The pressure for profits became greater and greater as the superstar began to look more like a black hole. The jerks used creative accounting and neat methods like "holding their feet to the fire" on the remnants of what had been a team of people. It finally culminated in the jerks being fired and my moving in as president of my original company. What a great deal. I now reported to the corporate president and chairman of the board.

The first 2 months I had the job, the order-cancellation rate exceeded the order-input rate for the superstar division. We were losing big dollars. The previous leaders had demonstrated to the rank and file that it was okay to, shall we say, cut corners.

We did all the dirty rotten things one has to do to survive a losing situation. We laid off and terminated all absolutely nonessential people. I cut my and my staff's salary 10 percent. We cut nonunion wages on a sliding scale dependent upon wage levels, trying to protect as much as possible the lower-end people. We cut off the air conditioning and opened the windows. We formed scrap committees and product improvement groups and made sure they contained the shop floor people.

We went by the book and were honest with the people. We renegotiated the first UAW giveback in the area. We fought hard and looked for the problem areas. We found it in pricing. The hotshots in their greatness overlooked a component of direct labor cost called cost-of-living allowance. A slight $2 per hour oversight. God were we shipping products with dollar bills stuck in the ports. So out to the customers with 20 to 30 percent price increases in a depressed market. Talk about verbal abuse, did we get it, and from some real pros.

After losing $2.5 million, we made a profit fully 2 months before I'd predicted we would. It felt so good I cried. We would survive, and I knew the verbal abuse from the president would stop.

At this juncture, another merger took place. Our corporation was acquired by a holding company, and corporate had acquired another division. I had a new direct boss from corporate now, one who had come with the newly acquired division. We were making money.

We continued to improve operations and I now had money for capital expenditures. The newly acquired division was performing poorly. My new boss was supposed to integrate the divisions, but was already retired. He was a (expletive deleted) of a good golfer and with good reason. He had lots of practice.

Corporate fired one VP and retired my boss, the other operational VP. I was invited to ascend to corporate as vice president of domestic operations. I hesitated. I enjoyed what I was doing. All I knew about corporate was that they controlled the purse strings, made up the rules, worked by the numbers, beat you if you missed them, and raised them if you made them. It's best summed up by the name I'd given the company plane, *The Sea Gull*. That's because they'd fly in the morning, (expletive deleted) all over you, and fly out in the evening. Also, the president was a mean drunk. And he did drink. But (expletive deleted), the dollars looked good. I was flattered. They talked about possibly moving me to president of corporate, and I really thought I could help do a job with the various plants, people, and divisions.

So I moved into the rarified atmosphere of corporate. What a wonderful place it was. Beautiful office with the most breathtaking views. Don't like the furniture? We'll have it fixed. Here's the selection of pictures, and if those aren't right, we can get something else. Someone doesn't like it that his secretary has to walk five offices down to the Xerox machine? Put in one for her. After years of trying to scrimp and save dollars for the company, it was appalling to see how it was pissed away at corporate.

I quickly observed the old boy routine. My boss was seldom there, as he was active on many boards of various companies and organizations. Large corporate donations were made to the various fund drives that he or his buddies were involved in. And back at the plants, on your hands and knees, they might give you some dollars for your local fund drives, if they approved it. The argument being that corporate can get more mileage out of the contributions they make. Obviously, "Corporate knows best in everything" was believed and practiced.

I now had four divisions, plus the communication and management information systems groups reporting to me with eight to ten plants in the United States. Starting out, I visited all of the plants and sat in on the weekly divisional meetings, and I was trying to develop a feel for the people and their problems and abilities without imposing myself on them. Back at the office, I was attempting to look at long-range strategies and opportunities. That didn't last very long. My boss chewed me out for not being out in the plants more. I didn't want to run them or have the managers feel I was looking over their shoulders to second-guess them. Too much corporate is counterproductive. You waste everyone's time.

The whispers went back to corporate that I was being hard on people in a key plant and not diplomatic. These people were $80,000 a year politicians.

We had eight plants, five divisions, no one talked to anyone else, and they all wanted equipment to do the same work their sister plants could do for them. I organized a managers' tour so the general and plant managers could get together and tour each others' plants and see what they could do for one another. Then I did the same with the engineering groups. We did get some cross-linking and a better attitude of helpfulness to each other.

A blow, the president moved up to become the holding company president and chairman, and the vice president of finance became president of corporate. He got concerned about plant utilization. That was the buzzword. He wanted me to move around some product lines. He was being fed lies by a money- and power-hungry general manager. I disagreed and defended my reasons for not wanting to do it. But I told him, even though I disagreed and the numbers supported me, if that's what he wanted me to do, I'd do it.

That was my mistake. In all my time in and around our company, I had not found out the basic tenet that the corporate bosses worked under; that is, "I don't make decisions. I only approve them." The utter simplicity of it is wonderful. You always keep someone between you and the decision. Thus, if it goes wrong, you can blame it on them saying, "I was just backing him!"

And here I was trying to force a corporate-raised cat to make a decision. He fired me. But then I'd restructured the U.S. operation, so they really didn't need me.

By the way, the move was made. It hasn't worked. Two divisions lost a portion of their profitability, the division manager didn't make his bonus, and it is rumored they want to move the product line elsewhere. The corporate president did fine, his bonus and stock options were great, and the company staggers forward.

I'm happy wearing my many hats in the small company I'm part of. My many skills serve us well as do my many friends. Remember, company loyalty is a one-way street in corporate America.

MEANINGS AND LESSONS

Jack finally caught on to the game, "I don't make decisions. I only approve them."

LESSON

Big dumb is when there are buffers between the jerks at the top and everybody below. Little dumb is when most employees are exposed to the jerk virus without protection.

We've just compared the command and control management model—still alive and well—with those newer today models, which can be described this way: "I'm doing two peoples' work, I have no time for my family, I have to watch my back, or I'll be run over."

We'd like you to notice that something very interesting has been happening in some of our contemporary organizations. You might have already caught it where you work, particularly if you're employed by a corporation where "big dumb" is the name of the game. Flatter hierarchies. Teams. You can guess what it means. Big dumb is becoming little dumb as the buffers (typically middle management) are being removed.

Think about that in terms of this story and others. If, for example, the manager without buffers or the team leader is a jerk, everybody interacting with them will feel it, directly and immediately. That is one reason you feel stressed. Look at Jack's story again. There are no Jacks to protect and understand you. You're being exposed to the hotshots, the drunks, the nitpickers, and the clever politicians. To be fair, however, you may be lucky and inherit an honorable, compassionate, highly people-skilled manager or team leader. And you will grow! Research shows there are not enough of these good individuals.

There is more that Jack tells us. There was loyalty in some divisions and plants. He implies there was a sense of fellowship and trust in places. The separateness led to both good and bad outcomes. Some managers cheated, some were lazy, and many were not held accountable for anything but dollar performance no matter how it was obtained. Corporate couldn't see beyond the bottom lines and the beautiful views from their perch.

LESSON

In the absence of corporatewide values, there will be inspired and rotten management. Heaven help the poor soul who gets stuck with "sea gull management" (fly in, dump your load, and fly away) and doesn't learn from the experience.

A clear picture is given of the way the two sets of leaders—hotshots from the east coast and the homegrown holding company—could care less about people. The first group sounds blatantly stupid and the second reprehensibly decadent, playing the game of boards and charity, drunk or sober, on or off the golf course, in or out of a company jet.

Let's give Jack's insight a "now" construction. A current management buzzword is "vision," but even better, "shared vision." That assumes a set of common beliefs and an almost equivalent perception about life, work, and family. Specifically, quality products can be a shared vision. So too can superior customer service. And fast, sustained growth. And being the best. And what about encouraging creativity, mutual support, cooperation? The concept is smart, but only in the sense that it's a wonderful goal. The execution—how to get it to happen—is dumb. Why? Because, once again, human nature at work cannot cooperate.

LESSON

Shared visions, in spite of all the hype, are not possible until people step into one another's shoes.

With people fighting to hold on to what they have, how many will have the inclination to see work through another's eyes?

Jack knows he didn't fit the culture he became a key part of. He never felt himself to be a true insider. But he did enjoy its trappings, the inspiring views, the "may I empty your ashtray, carry your bags, sir" service. But was he ever accepted? When asked, he said "no." He was always the visitor who never learned to say, "Yes, make mine a double."

YOU KILLED MY IDENTITY

During battles and in hostage-taking situations, snipers play a key role. They dispose of their targets with deadly, near silent efficiency. Someone standing next you is suddenly gone.

Managed-care leaders, whatever else you may think of them, are sharpshooters. Enter Fannie, a warmhearted, dedicated nurse of 30 years who was efficiently shot down in a different kind of war, waged to reduce overhead. Fannie is 62 and left the field after 28 gratifying years and 2 loathsome, frightening, depression-inducing ones. She is a bright, red-cheeked, sparkling-eyes type. We imagine patients love to see her enter their rooms. She wears good perfume, and you know when she's around.

Her husband, John, is an executive vice president of a supplier to the automotive industry. He realizes Fannie is troubled, that her identity and morale have been deeply shaken, but doesn't know what to do. He's angrier than she, sometimes even explosive about what's been happening in the healthcare industry. They are a close couple with three grown children and a 40-year marriage. We're in their Eden Prairie, Minnesota, home, comfortable and secure, full of books, records, and CDs. Names and places have been changed.

Well, it started out with a small clinic with multispecialty clinics. It was the best one in town. We had two hospitals run by different groups. Changes in healthcare came with the insurance being very expensive, and they decided they had to do something. Insurance wasn't paying for many procedures such as transplants because they were experimental.

They [insurance companies] got so upset with the physicians' charges that they decided to put a price on everything the physician would charge. And the hospitals got so they weren't filing reimbursements properly and the doctors were taking less. Insurance wouldn't pay except for so many days. I mean an appendectomy was overnight practically, babies were overnight, all that kind of stuff. They closed down half a hospital. All surgery was done at the Catholic hospital, so they got all the surgical beds. They had a heart clinic so all the heart people went over there. Pretty soon, we had a merger run by the same board.

I mean, when you think you are working for a nice place that cares about you, all of a sudden it's run by people you don't know. Your job is so different. The morale of the people working there was bad; changes were made. They tried to modernize at the same time with computers.

They gave me two doctors to work for instead of one. And I would answer all the phone calls, make all the appointments, assist the doctor with what he needed, talk to him about what he wants to do with the phone calls, call the pharmacies, call the patients back— do all that kind of stuff—plus documenting, and it was getting to be very difficult.

Because of all the stuff going on at the higher levels, their changes made it difficult for the people that were down below. Even nurses. I did very little nursing. It was just a shame. I didn't have time enough to talk to the people, to reassure them, which is what I've always done. It became hell, really.

The fellow that came and made all those changes was fired, although he said he resigned, but he was asked to leave. The hospitals couldn't do what this guy was hired to do, so he was outta' there. They had a contract but had to renege on it and go back to how it was to begin with.

They still have the same computer. I never had the time to learn it. It wasn't nursing the way I was used to it. So therefore, I chose to leave. The doctor I worked for was 2 years younger than me and asked if I'd stick with him until he left. And I said, "Yeah, I could do that." But actually I couldn't. I just couldn't.

Now they're hiring people with masters and PhDs in nursing to administrate. Nobody really likes what's going on. None of the nurses do. And every time I meet one, "Oh, you're so lucky you got out of there when you did." I guess the thing is to let nurses nurse. We haven't been able to do that. You know, if the physician is busy, he doesn't sit down at the bedside and talk things over. He answers questions but he doesn't really sit down and say this is what's going on. People would ask me questions and I could tell them.

MEANINGS AND LESSONS

John reports that Fannie has lost interest in most things, sits in the house, and phones their children. He has encouraged her to volunteer, but she makes only halfhearted attempts. She eats too much. He can "bring her around" by taking her on business trips, but between times he feels she still mourns for her life that died.

Fannie is depressed about not being a nurse. She knows it.

John knows it. The culture change Fannie experienced was culture shock. Culture shock is what most healthcare professionals are living through because for every Fannie there are countless others who now work for managed care.

LESSON

You are what you do, and when that identity is taken away, you're no longer the same person. Who are you?

Before the merger of the two hospital and clinic systems, Fannie was in her culture and the culture was in Fannie, in what she did, and how she did it. It was synergistic. Using this story as a model case, what we see is that when synergy is destroyed, the person and culture crack. Nothing remains the same. When the administrator was fired, the challenge of the new leaders was not to find a way to go back, but to find a way to go forward as if a new culture already existed. That it doesn't exist is due to the dumbness of administrators, like the man Fannie describes, who know nothing about culture or loyalty and can't understand that they are inseparable.

LESSON

It's as if managed care has split an atom whose radiation effects now blanket the country.

CAN'T RIDE WITHOUT A TICKET

David woke up to find himself working around people who looked familiar, but when he approached them, they didn't seem to know who he was. The offices looked like his company but were different—more worn and dusty. He wanted to get outdoors to clear his head but found that all the doors were locked. David's world had become a setting for *The Prisoner.* He's a marketing professional employed by a big city transportation system, a bright baby boomer in full bloom, confident, optimistic, and cynical. On top of that, he's good looking and fit. He's providing an insider's view of a large municipal public agency whose culture, whatever it used to be in its heyday, has become dumb and dumber. We're in a New England bookshop café. Names and places have been changed.

In my immediate job, from what I see—I'm a marketing professional and I'm pretty good at it—the old regime recognized that and allowed us to do our jobs. The new regime that's been retrofitted isn't interested in marketing. They're putting all their effort into controlling the media and what the media prints and reports on what the agency's doing.

So during all these months, they looked at me really skeptically. They thought that this was some kind of inside job. We were just funneling money to our friends. We weren't really producing anything. And so during that time, the last 12 months, I ferreted out a couple of projects that they wanted done. They wanted a new in-house newsletter, so I took that project on. And every 4 weeks, I come out with a new newsletter that's distributed to thousands of employees. I actually had to start that from scratch. I wrote all of it in the beginning. Now I have a couple of people I work with who contribute and I have a distribution system so we go out to about over a hundred different work sites. They wanted to do things their own way. So I allowed them to fail.

Modern companies are marketing driven. They know what their customer wants and needs, and they make decisions accordingly. The agency has historically been "build it and they will come." People used to come because they didn't have any choice. And today, they come only when it's beneficial. The bureaucracy decided not to pay any attention to what the customers were looking for. They oftentimes were logistics people from the military. They ran vehicles, tanks, and trains before. Now they run trains and buses.

My marketing head is a couple of years older than me; he's been here since he was 17. He's a dope. But he's kissed the right butts and clung on and done the right things for enough people to hold onto his position. He is now the marketing manager and has virtually no marketing instincts. He's marginally intelligent. He's screwing-up so much right now. Basically, what happened, the old marketing department was let go except this guy. He was little more than a paper shuffler. A new regime came in who had no ability to hire anyone. This guy pleaded to be manager, and he knows only the transit system. Then, another regime came in with a budget and started hiring for his department. Now the guy has a little empire. He makes presentations to bus garage managers, people who don't know marketing.

I've seen the posting for the job under him and they're asking for someone who knows a lot more than him. I'd be happy to be the head of marketing. He's not a team builder; I'm a team builder. I would love to have that job. Actually, I'd love to have that job somewhere else because I don't think it's ever going to happen here. The way he got the job was politically astute. He knew where the money was. He went for the money. He never brought an original idea to the table. He sucks up other people's ideas and brings them in.

His people don't talk among themselves. A lot of people take extended lunches and really don't do much. He and one of his guys produce a map every 6 months. And the map is a big deal. He doesn't do the work. He just lost his main person because you get sick of doing every one else's job.

We have over a million riders each day. I put a program together to teach people about the new card system, and they spent all kinds of money on it, but I never got as much as a thank you.

Here's another good example. They wanted to use all the internal photographers we had. I knew that they were completely unreliable because I had tried previously. When they asked me about them, I told them the truth. They didn't believe me. I let them find out for themselves how unreliable and unprofessional they were. And meanwhile, I had previously built up a team, a few people that I work with. Some on the inside, some on the outside. As opportunities arose, I would offer a suggestion, but I would never tell them what to do. I would offer this as a possible solution. And I told them what the outcome would be, the cost, and the quality of the deliverable product. And in the beginning, they would say, no, no, no. Lately I hired an outside firm to produce our television spots, which are running right now. And then I worked with an outside person to create the back of the buses right now.

The head of purchasing knew that we had to do a lot of creative work for the launch of our new token system. We've spent $75 million. They told us that the head of purchasing wanted to help out. They contacted my boss and they started a procedure several months ago to hire an outside firm to assist on design work. Meanwhile, we already had an outside firm with a design contract. My manager, not wanting to cause any problems, went along with the head of purchasing to initiate the purchase of a service to do design work for us. So he asked me to help write the specifications for this job. Months went by and I was on the selection committee. We were already using the original design firm and I was overloaded with work. But this thing that was initiated several months earlier finally had come to a decision-making mode even though at this point it was already moot. My vice president asked me why I was out of the office at a really busy time, and I said that based on my manager's request, I was one of the evaluators on something that should have been thrown in the garbage 3 months earlier. He said, "Well, that's ridiculous." He says, "Of course we're not going to use them. Who told you to do that?" I said, "The head of purchasing did."

MEANINGS AND LESSONS

Power, position, favors, hanging on, making no waves, riding the ripples so as to remain visible—ah, the sweet smell of the smell. Toadies with connections and no brains can win (David's manager), toadies with connections and brains can also win (choose among confidants/advisers of U.S. presidents, governors, or mayors as you wish), but toadies with no connections, smart or dumb, can't win.

It's easy to visualize David's boss, puffed up and sitting in the organization sun making scratch marks on a log pretending they are real words conveying real messages. How can you be afraid of a toad that's somehow assumed the size and shape of a human being? Of course people who work for a toad will take long lunch hours and do little work.

LESSON

Take the egos that need massaging out of your organization, and toadies will never again rise to power.

David shows us the maneuvering required to get work done in a large bureaucracy, the kind often headed by the well-connected. For example, to get the right work to happen—his photographer story—the wrong work has to happen first. To kill a project that shouldn't have been started in the first place (yet could proceed under everyone's nose)—the outside supplier of design work—David had to expose the director of purchasing's blunder.

The errors made by people with no talent and no motivation beyond what's required to keep themselves supplied with every comfort constitute a common failure of bureaucracies. David's example reads like small potatoes compared with the miscalculations and arrogance of the world's huge toadies. Military leaders who've squandered millions of lives are excellent examples. They are documented precisely by Geoffrey Regan in *The Book of Military Blunders* (Santa Barbara, ABC-CLIO, 1991).

Comparing the military fool with David's boss is like comparing a galaxy to a sun, but there are common properties: David says of his leader, "He's a dope. But he's kissed the right butts and clung on . . . He's marginally intelligent." Regan says of Marshal Budënny, Stalin's friend and one of the few survivors of the Red Army purge:

> Marshal Semyon Mikailovich Budënny's claim to being the most incompetent commander in this whole book is a strong one . . . Against the Germans in 1941 he suffered probably the biggest defeat ever suffered by any general in military history. Already senile at 58, Budënny commanded the Russian forces in the Ukraine and Bessarabia. . . . Even though he outnumbered the Germans three or four to one in men and tanks . . . Runstedt and Kleist ran rings around him. Budënny's incompetence cost the Russians 1,500,000 men.

Real lives lost are not equivalent to poor decision making, incompetence, and ignorance. But to emerge as a major dumbhead who might some day lose lives, one has to start somewhere. Budënny had minor jobs before Stalin picked him. David's boss also had a small job. But who knows to what high position he might rise where great damage could be done to others?

LESSON

Being promoted above one's level of competence implies some talent to start with. But promoting inherent incompetence, ah, that's the stuff of dumb leadership.

HE DOESN'T KNOW PEOPLE

It hurts to see a once-profitable organization whose employees you care about and trust, one you've given your life to—rising from sales trainee to CEO—become petty, uncaring, selfish, and unprofitable. It hurts more when you are part of the group who selected an unfeeling, gluttonous engineer for president. Adam, the man we're visiting, is contrasting his management style with that of the CEO he helped select.

Adam is retired, in his early seventies, and on the board of the company he headed for 25 years. We're in his home in northern Indiana, a rambling tudor style house backing against a stand of trees. He's a widower. There are pictures of his wife, children, and grandchildren all over his study. Adam is a tall, soft-spoken man who exudes Mr. Honesty. You feel he'd like to embrace you. We like him. He loves to play golf and is actively involved in many charitable organizations. Places and names have been changed.

> I started off as trainee in sales, made the sale, went back, changed clothes, made the sample, changed clothes again, and brought back the sample to the customer we were trying to develop for testing. Just did everything for them. Finally, I had to make a decision whether I should stay in sales or stay in production. They convinced me to stay in production because of the fact that I get along well with people. I was plant superintendent. We had 90 people. Years later, I became vice president. Then the president had a heart attack and I became president. We were doing $9 or $10 million in sales, now more than $60 million but we're not profitable. I remained

president for 21 years. I retired and stayed on as a consultant for 7 years and now I'm on the board.

Yes, it is true. I like everybody. I say yes and admit I like everybody until I find they don't meet up to my expectations. Then I don't dislike them, but I just don't have anything else to do with them. That's all. I don't like to be used. I want people to be as fair to me as I am to them. If that's a fault, it's one I enjoy. It's easier to be nice to people than to insult them or to hurt them. It's a lot easier.

As the president of the company, I became involved. I was very involved with the employees. I spent a lot of time out in the plant everyday. I always took a walk through the plant everyday, saying hello to the employees, making sure that people knew that someone was interested in what they were doing.

I think one of the things that the new president lacks is that trait. He didn't, and still doesn't, spend enough time out in the plant. He never got as well acquainted with employees as he should.

Once there was talk that we might have a strike there because we were in the midst of negotiations. And I had a lot of people in the plant who I knew well and who came to me. Part of the problem was the lack of interest by management in the employees. They felt that management wasn't interested in what they did, how they did it, and so forth. That's what they indicated. Yes, there's always money on the table. But the fact that we were able to communicate and develop a relationship meant we never did have to go to a strike threat. The employees were disillusioned and felt they were not part of the family.

I think part of the problem is they developed teams of management people. What they called the "big five" and the "elite five" and so forth. The people kind of resented this. That group seemed to have all the control and paid no attention to or gave credit to anyone else involved. The president didn't become aware of what was going on and missed this entirely.

My theory of running an operation was customers, profits came first. But their theory is volume. Increase that volume. Growth was great for 10 years. We increased our business almost threefold but started losing money doing so.

The president is a type of guy who does not follow through on what his managers do. I think it's inherent in a person. He never had any involvement in the city. He doesn't belong to any organizations. He's just totally too private. I think his friendships were very limited. It's just his personality. I don't think his personality is leadership material. There's nothing mean about the guy; he's just a very private person. His direction is very narrow. More volume.

How they're treating people? He does not get involved with that which I feel is necessary. Probably in larger companies people don't get involved in the day-to-day stuff. But I grew up in a small company and it was my way of operating.

I think whatever you do, you do it correctly. High quality, customer satisfaction. Now they inspect the quality into the product rather than making a quality product. It's costly. To me, you have to catch quality at the source of manufacturing, not at the shipping door.

My advice would be, "Get out in the plant; get involved. Direct. You're supposed to be directing the people. Get more involved with them. Don't wait until it's all happened." He says, "Yeah, yeah, yeah." Now the board's putting pressure on him to get profitable.

MEANINGS AND LESSONS

How a total culture can change with a change in top leadership personality is what Adam's story is about. The two protagonists in this tidy tale represent contrasting corporate value systems being debated today: prudence versus expansion, involvement versus detachment, generosity versus selfishness, caring versus coldness, citizenship versus estrangement, trust versus resentment. Whither corporate America?

We hear about a management team that distanced itself from employees and were the elitists of the plant. Quality problems had to be caught at the end of the manufacturing process. There was the threat of a strike. Adam wants the president to be "involved" (his favorite word) but can't convince him. The president has other ideas.

═══════════════════════════════════════

LESSON

Selecting a dumb-with-people president can happen in a small or large company. Both suffer: the large ones in public, the small in anonymity.

═══════════════════════════════════════

The emergence of the "big five" is a result of the president's style of noninvolvement. Adam's use of that phrase (also the "elite five") is proof of his identification with the workers and their resentment. Elitist defines that part of the president's character Adam doesn't directly touch, in fact tends to deny by saying, "There's nothing mean about the guy." Adam, who likes everybody, can't bring himself to excoriate the man who wiped out the decency of the culture.

Adam's company is tightly held. There's minimal accountability so long as there are profits. The concern, according to Adam, isn't the president's style; it's losing money. But here's a paradox, speaking of style and profits. Where have we run into the trait of detachment before? What can be satirically referred to, as Adam does, as being "a very private person" is a characteristic shared by leaders in other stories. In the eyes of some, that trait (don't get too close to the people) is a virtue guaranteeing objectivity in creating profit. Adam hints that the president should be in a bigger company.

The president is depicted as a "could-be, should-be" guy—wrong place, wrong time. He's become somewhat of a laughing stock, a slowly failing leader upon whom pressure is finally being applied but for the wrong reasons.

BOMBING RUN

The fighter plane banked low over the woods and made a run toward a camouflaged field. The pilot pulled the bomb control lever and watched as two puffs of smoke marked the spot where he had obliterated the buildings. World War II? Central America? No, third generation playing war with the family inheritance. The first generation worked hard and prospered, the second sat on it, and the third liked airplanes and squandered it.

Lewis, the general manager of one of the few remaining plants not yet bombed, tells the story. He's a large, careworn man leading a beaten-up army off the field. He's talking about how it was and what happened to a once-proud force. We arranged a brief meeting with him in a Chicago restaurant. He can't stay long because they'll be looking for him. Names and places have been changed.

I just got a call from a recruiter, but at my age, I can't take the job. My company is a 90-year-old family company begun in Chicago. We were basically quick turnaround black-and-white printers. I've been with the company for 45 years.

It started with a summer job. Graduated from high school. Joined the service. Met my wife at the company. Went to night school. I was in customer service and sales. What I've seen is that the first generation are innovators, the second generation are caretakers, and the third generation throw it away. We've gone from the second generation making $60 million to the third generation making $15 million. The third generation closed its eyes and didn't believe there would be change. Their answer was to cut everything. We had 300 employees. We now have fewer than 60. Copy machines and computers had a big impact on the industry. Other printers came into our field. They eventually went bankrupt. Everything stayed status quo, and we didn't develop new markets. They cut everything to maintain profit for the family.

Management style? There wasn't any. They hardly talked to the employees. The owners complained to management about costs. Wanted big markups and profits. Many people left. Five years ago, he asked me to be the general manager of the operation. I went home that night, and in the car I said to myself, rationally, "There's no decision here. Don't take it. This is a dead animal. You'll kill yourself trying to breathe life into it." Emotionally, I said, "Well, I've been with this company 38 years and I'm going to have that job." So, it was an emotional decision, not a rational decision. For the first couple of years, I pumped it up a little bit. They gave me some bonuses. I tried to make some changes. We still maintain a good product. As long as I produced profit, he didn't bother me. I have a strong feeling for the family. They have a big pride. They want to keep it going. They're all independently wealthy.

Definitely it could have been saved. It should've been like the first generation—better ideas and spend some money instead of amass bigger profits. Be innovative. We, the company, are survivors. We own all our lands, buildings, and equipment. Never mortgaged or leveraged anything. A lot of printers went out of business in the 1990s.

Biggest mistake: not to spend money. They just try to put it all in their pockets. Not have trust. They never trusted each other or their employees. Not listen to the marketplace. No pensions. The first generation was very benevolent. That man worked hard to keep out the unions by paying higher than union wages, better benefits, everything. We still give out a turkey at Thanksgiving.

What's the lesson? Get some people underneath you that you can talk to and listen to them. Finance, marketing, and production. Pay the price for them and listen to them. You have to spend money to make money. You can't just put it away. Be trustworthy of your people and your family.

MEANINGS AND LESSONS

The story is more about Lewis and why he stays than it is about a failing family business. There he is, Lewis, the devoted retainer who can be counted on to turn out the lights. While the heirs play, Lewis gathers together what few employees remain, rallies their spirits—"we still give out a turkey"—and squeezes out a nickel in profit.

The loyal employee clinging to a corporate family no matter how dysfunctional is more a story of yesterday than today. Forty years—part of the company's growth, its decline, and hanging in trying to resurrect it before the last hurrah. Why should Lewis want to protect the lavish lifestyles of the third generation?

One reason is Lewis rose above his station and feels privileged to be part of a small-potatoes aristocracy. Notice the "we" in talking about his company's ownership of land, buildings, and equipment. (We expected to hear next that the family opened its estate to visitors.) He mentions the family's wealth and pride. While not personally wealthy, he too has pride in the family name and identifies strongly with the founder. Lewis had his values and identity formed by life in the company. You never get that formative influence out of your system.

LESSON

When you've lived your life in one company and the president shouts "charge," you'll pick yourself up for a final effort because to die anyplace else but under the corporate flag is unthinkable.

FACES
OF DUMBNESS

THE PUZZLE
OF TEAMS

Teams can be collectively dumb even when their members are individually smart. Dumb teams are seldom described in the literature. And the smart teams that are described are not smart for very long. A self-directed or leader-directed group that is struggling to cooperate is far from a team. Their attempts are painful to watch. "What went wrong?" we ask.

They answer, "We weren't sure what to do. We didn't like the leader. There was no trust. All the teams began to compete. It was the same old system with a new name. Management didn't ask us. What do they expect? It saves money for the company; everybody soon caught on to that."

Can teams be saved? The answer is yes, but saved to what purpose? What is management's understanding when it mandates teams? We'll unravel the puzzle in two ways. The first is related to management's inadvertent stumbling into the grossest of errors known to all philosophers beginning with Aristotle. It's a common intellectual trap, one instinctively understood even by children.

It is confusing the ideal conception—the image of the self-directed team—with reality—self-directed teams in fact. Management has a picture in its head that ultimately appears on a computer screen. It's a beautiful and clean picture, reinforced by thoughts of democracy and empowerment. Unfortunately, that picture has little representation in the real world, yet thousands of managers and employers behave as if it does. The most primitive of peoples know the phenomenon. It's called magic.

The second answer to the puzzle is more contemporary and more comfortable for most of us, having to do with the psychology of expectations and relationships.

1. It might have been more productive for industry if employees had been forbidden to form teams. Tell people not to do something—it started with the apple—and they will do it. For example, there might not have been a Revolutionary War in this country if King George III and his generals had insisted the colonists start a revolution—get self-directed.

   The words "self-directed" sound so democratic and vigorous, how can it fail? But unfortunately, like too many management ideas, it's an imposed one, not arrived at spontaneously and naturally, and that's one reason there is failure. It's unrealistic to expect to wipe away decades of other-directed learning by blowing reveille and yelling, "Now hear this!"

2. Leaders aren't factoring in the complexities of human nature as much as they should be. Surely they must remember how it was when they were young and their parents insisted on something being "good for you."

3. Leaders confuse management books with reality. If the real-world effort falls short of what the book describes, management blames itself, tries again, fails again, and is weakened by a misguided attempt to reconcile the irreconcilable.

4. The wonderment is not why teams fail but why some succeed. They're fighting ambivalent feelings and fast-shifting expectations. The need to protect one's job collides with a sincere desire to help the organization.

The interplay of three factors helps explain the team puzzle: (1) the values with which we've been raised, (2) the true nature of corporate goals, and (3) global marketing strategies.

From Family, to School, to Work, and Back Again

Picture yourself entering kindergarten, your parents words in your head, "Be nice, be cooperative, share things." You soon discover that other children, instructed the same way, are not nice, cooperative, or willing to share. Teachers try to create harmony and mostly fail.

A few years pass and you're on the way to high school. What you watch on TV is competition building to a crescendo of violence. The baseball, football, hockey, and basketball cards you collect are all about competition. In your athletic or academic groups, tough competitors are valued. You observe stars being born. Still later, you begin to be influenced by the hype surrounding superstars of sports and the media. If you happen to read about business heroes, they are seldom depicted as altruistic.

Now you're in the workplace, geared-up for success. What happens? You hear your parents again—be nice, be cooperative, share things. Find solutions through common effort. It's management telling you to get into a team-building mode, to help your colleagues, and not to worry about individual glory. It will all work out and rewards will be shared.

Your parents were right all the time. It's a culture conflict. The psychology doesn't fit, with first one identity and then another. The sociology doesn't fit, with first one group value and then another. It's nightmare time. Mother says cooperate, society says compete, the organization says cooperate. Where do you put your faith? You've entered the world of business where little seems to stay the same for very long.

TEAM DECISION MAKING?

A Madison, Wisconsin, newsletter's letter to the editor expresses a paradox about teams.

My company is finally catching up with modern management: team decision making! Until recently, major decisions were made by individuals, mostly after consulting with those most impacted by the decision and with those having insights and the suitable knowledge and experience. Sometimes people were upset about not being consulted. Sometimes decisions weren't necessarily the best ones. Sometimes bad decisions could have been good ones if the proper person would have been involved. Therefore, it's no wonder that team decision making (we call it TDM) seemed the thing to do.

Our major competitor, we were told, has been using TDM. Our chief executive became convinced that we also need to embrace the concept. After a bunch of consultants spent a week with us, we're now blessed with the ability to use teams for any major decision.

Not only will our decisions be better, but more of our colleagues will feel that they are playing a greater role in the company's future. Empowerment. That's the word everyone uses.

Great stuff, this TDM! I haven't seen a bad decision yet. In fact, I haven't seen a good decision either. There have been *no* decisions. I'm exaggerating, there have been a few, but they've all been minor ones.

The teams I've been on reach consensus through discussion and votes. However, there's an underlying activity. Some people wouldn't dare present an opinion, or vote on an issue, in the presence of people with power over them who would frown on their opinion or vote. Many people vote according to how the outcome would influence *them,* not the company. Discussions, however, focused on company issues. However, what *wasn't* discussed seemed to be the force that drove consensus.

As I said, most of the important decisions haven't yet been made. These are matters that would have been quickly dispensed with prior to TDM. The issues sure have been talked about, though. It takes teams to decide who should be on a team. It takes meetings to learn about the issues. Sometimes, a consensus doesn't drive a decision because an important person may not agree with the consensus. He, then, delays signing off on the decision and plays games to push the team to agree with him. For instance, one director just held a meeting to show us a business magazine's article on how a decision, similar to the one our team agreed to, turned out poorly. The relevance of the article to our situation, however, was weak at best.

It's difficult to get anything done with all the meetings we attend each week. To help out, we use company e-mail. Everyone on a team e-mails their opinions to the other team members. Responses are e-mailed to all. Sure saves on meeting space! But I dread logging on to the computer: message after message—and most are worthless, many are long, and several specifically ask for my response. This "discussion" can drag out for months.

I don't mean to be rude, but the only people who like this "empowerment" are the people who most likely wouldn't have been consulted in the old autocratic system. They haven't at all influenced—except by voting along with their leader—any decision.

I'd love to be on a team with the assignment to report on the success of TDM.

Anonymous
from *Innovative Leader,* Vol. 6, No. 7, 1997

HIS PEOPLE AREN'T READY

The road to self-directed team hell can be paved with good intentions. Our warrior, Tom, goes into his corporate battle prepared to give everything because he knows the objective is right. We run into him walking through the exhibits of a lavishly presented electronics manufacturing equipment convention. Money is everywhere. Tom stood out at last year's team-building workshop. He's fortyish, a plant manager, very energetic, and assertive. He is loyal to his nationally known electronics company and about to purchase a $1 million piece of equipment. Was he on a roll!

We judge him against his peers. He's a prime candidate for being stolen away from his employer. But he likes his southwestern lifestyle and wants to stay. He would ride a motorcycle through a hoop of fire if it would make teams happen for him. We listen very carefully. Names and places have been changed.

This story is about the desire to have self-managed or self-directed work cells. In order to do that, you have to give people the tools they need to be able to do the tasks that need to be done within the group. They sort of take on different roles to be able to handle their self-directed cells.

We have a struggle. We try to do this to relinquish more of the managerial role to the people. Some of them begin to take large advantage of that. And even though you try to get them to feel committed to a team, some of them will take advantage of their new authority.

It's not easy. [laughs] Let's put it that way. Oh, I think I have a real desire to have my team succeed. It might start out very simple, like scheduling your own vacation, break times, making sure there is enough shift coverage. If the team is strong enough, they can hire and fire. They can give each other appraisals of performance. And they might even do budgeting.

But they need certain social skills that they may not have. They need certain business skills that they may not have. It's a long process and a hurting process. All that for someone to relinquish to get into a training mode to allow them to do those things that normally would be done for them.

We do team awards rather than individual awards. So when a group of people accomplishes something that's above and beyond, you try and reward that kind of behavior and that's what I'm trying to do.

MEANINGS AND LESSONS

Tom didn't want to say anything more for the record. As we walked back on to the exhibits, he said he was organizing teams because he was told to. He wasn't happy, but it was his job and he was doing it as best he could. His people weren't ready for it. He thought more sophisticated machines would help since that would mean less reliance on people.

Tom's frustration doesn't dampen his zest for living or dampen the "high" he experiences purchasing newer technology for his plant. He's showing us reasons self-directed teams don't work. That knowledge bothers but doesn't stop him because he's also showing us the alternative—more sophisticated machines. That alternative may well be the fallout of the team fad—more challenges for engineers, software companies, and their respective suppliers.

What about the people currently in manufacturing? Some will rise to the level demanded by the technology, some will learn how to cooperate, and some will fly off their small universe and grab less demanding jobs. What's certain, as you read other stories of technological change, is that very little will remain the same. The smart people will grow and survive while the dumb will move down on the scale and run right into the underclass population moving up.

Lesson

If we can't teach production workers how to cooperate for their own good, there may be a glut of hamburger flippers, clerks, and telemarketers.

Tom has picked up the rock to reveal one underlying weakness in his company's ability to compete using home-grown talent. Outsourcing and going overseas are understandable alternatives. But it's a spotty picture. While Tom is an optimistic manager who is constantly challenging himself—a plus for his employer—his employees haven't yet caught fire. They are stuck in the pattern of competition, suspicion, and selfishness. There is no learning environment, except for Tom and perhaps others like him. Why he is different from his people is the question his company needs to address. We've raised that kind of question with other leaders, and their answers make sense. They don't know where to start. Is it really their problem or society's? If someone could tell them how to change old behavior patterns without breaking the bank, they would.

Lesson

Resistive employees give management the excuse to move production overseas. Optimistic, caring leaders may stem the tide.

THERE WAS NO REAL TEAM

Carolyn's three children know how to speak to one another, bathe, and dress themselves. So naturally, Carolyn, an adminis-

trative leader in an integrated hospital with about 4500
employees, assumed the same would be true of the employees she was supposed to weld into a team. She's a humorous,
energetic, tall woman who walks, talks, and gestures with a
purpose. She is an RN with a master's degree in business. Her
hospital had to change because the healthcare field changed.
She is selected to run a large unit and develop a system of
self-directed teams and has been trying to do a system
makeover for almost a year and a half. She sees little progress.
She talks about getting her people to begin speaking to one
another. She has insight into the weaknesses of employees
who are asked to move from one culture to another. We're in
her home in Phoenix. Names and places have been changed.

We're becoming very team-based. I think it's going to take years. I
lead the pilot unit where everybody has a different kind of job.
We've remodeled the nursing unit—it's clinically based—and all the
team members belong. For example, the nurse-manager only managed the nurses, and now I manage everybody there at that physical
place taking care of the patients. So I manage the housekeepers, the
respiratory therapists, the dietitian, the social worker, the case manager. It's all blended.

It is my role to clean up, to blend three nursing units. Those
folks would not attend a class together. They would not speak to
each other. And I was to turn them into one unit. [gestures with
exasperation] I started around Thanksgiving when they were supposed to be doing self-scheduling. This was the group of existing
nurse-managers, 3-to-11 shift managers, and 11-to-7 shift managers,
whom I asked to leave. Then I replaced all of them and began to
bring this workplace of 150 people together. Initially, truly, they
weren't speaking to one another. They didn't have the competencies
to work across units.

I'd say that teamwork was the issue. I mean, it didn't exist. It
was worse than nothing. It's only been 13 or 14 months, but finally
we are speaking and there are intangible things. People take classes
together; they've crossed over. They were supposed to be doing self-
scheduling. I didn't put them on one schedule because they weren't
even speaking. And I had one unit on Christmas day that, let us say,
should have had 15 people on. But they had done their own sched-

ule and turned it in to me, and I had one person who was willing to work on Christmas. And that's how they turned it in.

The assumption is that the patient will get more coordinated care. There's a three-person team that takes care of eight patients, and physically, they're in one hallway with one substation. What we're trying to do is change the way we think and the question should be: Did you not have to call us? We used to track the number of minutes it took to respond, and that would tell us if we were doing a good job. Everybody knows that everybody goes to the bathroom when they wake up in the morning. So we ought to, I think, anticipate that, and patients shouldn't have to call us. Should someone have to follow the lunch tray to make sure you really got a straw with the milk you ordered?

In my first staff meeting with these people, I told them I wasn't going to tolerate the use of the "F" word in the hallway or to the patient. Not one time, without exception. [gestures, making a speech] I have a policy that says they would not speak that way and I would not tolerate it. That was one of my first orders of business. And it's sort—it's a silly thing—and I told them that in my house with my children, we call those "plumber words." Actually, those were words my father used when he did plumbing, and that was the only time I was accustomed to hearing those words. And that's sort of my claim to fame there.

MEANINGS AND LESSONS

Carolyn doesn't have a team. Her employees give no input and are resistive. She is teaching them fundamentals and remaking the culture in her own image. The "F" word story symbolizes her approach, demonstrating that she's their boss in conduct and values.

The unexpected seems to be happening at her hospital, and it's a laugh on management theorists. The restructuring brought about by a team-based system has shaken loose new kinds of leaders, not team leaders, but command-control leaders with a heart. Carolyn, who is interpersonally skilled, has been given the opportunity to manage a segment of the hospital her way, and she's taken it.

Lesson:

If you combine command-control techniques with enlightened personal values, you can rise in the world of managed care.

Carolyn wants the self-directed concept to take hold but recognizes its limitations. Her organization has been wasting precious time chasing a concept out of harmony with employee values. The only winner may be Carolyn herself.

GOOD IDEAS FROM *THOSE* PEOPLE?

From the lips of a consultant, here's an insider's look at the rise and fall of a hospital team. Ken is a professional trainer with over 20 years of experience. He's a stocky man in his midforties, dark hair, a full square face, wearing blue jeans. It's Saturday afternoon in New York City and we meet at a bookstore on 82nd Street. Names and places have been changed.

> It was the CEO who began the project on cooperation and team building. This was an 800-bed university hospital in 1990. The project started at a high level with senior managers and vice presidents. And the CEO was the champion of this. When it moved down to a lower level, to the employee level, the manager of human resources and organizational development called me in to do team building, and that's what I did for 14 months. The CEO left to take a position in a hospital in California and my direct contact, the manager of human relations and organizational development, left to go to Minnesota. So that left the project without any internal support. And it certainly left me as an external consultant without a sponsor.
>
> A new CEO had been hired and she freezes things until she gets an opportunity to take a look at what was going on. I think other reasons were that some people were feeling threatened by the project because you had managers that had some of their inefficiencies being exposed by workers, and that put them in an uncomfortable and sometimes embarrassing position so that they certainly were not in favor of continuing this project. So it had a mixed reception. There were some managers who saw some value in this, but others who did not and felt very threatened by it.

The culture was throughout this whole thing very authoritarian. One of the senior vice presidents referred to the workers in this hospital as "the serfs," just to give you a reflection of it. There were some managers who were a bit more enlightened, but that was not typical. It was basically an authoritarian culture.

Serf referred pretty much to the unskilled workers, the housekeepers, people who worked in the garages, the runners, the people who delivered the supplies from the supply department to the nursing floors. I don't think he was referring to the skilled people but rather the unskilled workers.

We were able to put together a team process where people identified problems that were measurable. Part of their task was to document the problems in terms of whatever quantifiable elements they had and also measure the difference in the outcomes when a solution was implemented. We had hard data in dollars and cents to prove successes. But they did not want to continue even though we were able to translate improvements into monetary terms.

Sure, it was cultural. Sure. It was more than let's save money. It was a counterculture to an authoritarian system to empower people who normally didn't have any power. It was a very threatening thing. And that, in some people's minds, was even of greater importance than the money these people were able to save. I knew it right from the beginning. It was all very apparent.

The project scope was a trial. I only had 5 units out of 35 in the hospital. The teams varied from 5 or 6 and up to 12 depending on the nursing unit. It was a demonstration. It was to prove the point that these people could be greater contributors to the whole system if given the opportunity and the right circumstances. They had a lot more to offer than just the labor that they were there for.

The majority of the people who were really in power said no. Other people who were still in the ranks of senior managers but less powerful than the top level saw a lot of value. Head nurses saw value to this. So it wasn't 100 percent of everybody in this hospital condemning this. They tried to rally to my cause and failed. They sent memos and had meetings. There was that effort to try and preserve this. But they needed to have a champion who was going to make this system work. Without a champion, it could not stand in this kind of environment.

Of course I was disappointed. We worked very hard for 14 months to show the viability of this thing. I felt sorry for all these people who had worked hard on these teams for 14 months and now will be told it's ended, thanks very much, go back to work. Especially when they had started really coming together from various departments in terms of a cohesive whole and now had to go back to the old ways again. And then if anything was done later on, there would be this bad experience that would poison any future attempts.

I have a videotape of these teams at work, making presentations to management. Some people became more confident. They became more enthusiastic about their work. About the hospital. So we saw a lot of positive changes. I stayed in touch with people in the hospital.

You're asking about the lessons. Well, first of all, what we were really talking about was a culture change. And that can't happen without absolute commitment from the top-level people in that organization. We had that in the beginning. But when the CEO left, that top-level drive that was keeping this thing going was gone. And what it showed was something that was known for a long, long time. It's that you cannot create change in an organization without the absolute commitment of the senior leadership. We were able to be successful as long as senior leadership was there. When he left, it was gone. There was no CEO for a long time, and then a new CEO came in who did not support this because she was too new. We continued for a while, but it was struggling along because it had been given long-range funding for a period of 6 months. But there was no real enthusiasm behind it without a CEO who was pushing senior vice presidents underneath to do this.

There was a very authoritarian mind-set. That's their paradigm for how a hospital should be run. The CEO who was in favor of this was only there for 2 months. I was there another 12 after he left, fighting an uphill battle against people who didn't want to see this. When he left, all the energy to keep this thing going was gone. People with an authoritarian mind-set just reverted to type. And they were the ones who felt threatened and they were ones who felt embarrassed by this.

We did it right. I think we were just victimized by circumstances. Without the senior top leader making it happen, it falls off the plate. If he disappears, it falls off the radar screen. It doesn't exist anymore. And it just happened that this kept going on because nobody took the impetus to really end it. So it was kind of running on its own momentum and became a nuisance and annoyance. People stopped attending meetings and it slowly began to wither away until there was nothing viable left. And then a new CEO comes on board and it ends.

You have the manager of patient relations who finds this absolutely terrific. But who cares about her? She doesn't have a power job. We didn't have the VP of nursing—power. That's the power seat—yeah. She's uh, uh, we don't want this—no. So you got the guy who's responsible for the kitchen and he thinks it's a great idea. But who cares what he thinks? The unit managers were in favor of this. But the vice president of nursing didn't want to hear about it. She was overriding what her people were saying.

There's a lot of lessons here, but they're lessons that we knew about. But sometimes, things don't always work out the way you plan. You start a project in good faith and things change. You get people who leave and the whole dynamic of things changes around you. So what are you going to do? You hope and pray somebody will come in and champion this thing, but it doesn't happen.

MEANINGS AND LESSONS

Power is everything, and no matter what employees and managers feel about a program, it's going to disappear if leaders don't want it. This is not unusual in organizations, but Ken tells it well. We feel for him and the employees whose lights were turned off. The supremacy of power is the big story here, irresponsible power which in time can run amok and is difficult to contain.

Ken's program was like a lighthouse beam sweeping a dark sky. What had been previously hidden as it cut the darkness could be viewed if ever so briefly. Management saw the view too clearly. It revealed manager inefficiencies while employees created worthwhile, money-saving ideas. That was not how the power people wanted the world to look. The situation could be better controlled in darkness. So darkness returned.

LESSON

If you can't placate the power gods in an organization, you will be defenseless against their thunderbolts.

The success of a new program isn't assured even if your champion leading you through the woods is the CEO. When Ken's champion left, he was fair game. His teams had a lingering organizational death, longer than might have been the case if the transition to a new CEO hadn't occupied the key vice presidents. Ken's sorrow isn't fully expressed (he was telling the story 3 years after it happened), but empathy is easy. Team members were dropping dead around him. Minor players rallied to the cause but couldn't be heard. Better to have cut quickly and mercifully. The budget allowed it to bleed to death.

LESSON

Autocratic organizations like managed-care hospitals are as arrogant as ancient Rome and the sixteenth-century Catholic church, and if they don't change, they too are destined to bleed to death.

A final look at Ken's teams. Initially, they were infused with the energies of the CEO, the organizational development consultant, and Ken. In the dark night of that traditionally autocratic hospital, for a brief time it was, "Oh say can you see . . . " The teams tore into things and produced measurable, money-saving efficiencies. Ken ran meetings, and energy coursed through the groups. While not as miserable as Carolyn's "teams," Ken and Carolyn performed similar roles. They are both strong professionals who know what they want and function well as leaders. Those were not self-directed teams; they were strong, compassionate, leader-directed ones.

LESSON

If self-directed teams aren't working, dump them and bring in an outside leader-facilitator. There's no shame in changing the game plan.

IT'S RELATIONSHIPS, DUMMY!

People with PhDs are smart, right? Those with research PhDs are even smarter. It depends about what. Brain power, as in the following story, is no guarantee of team power. If you think brainy people struggled and clawed to get those hefty degrees just to give away good ideas to a team, where were you when, you know what.

We're in Dean's office overlooking his well-manicured corporate campus. Dean is calm. It's a beautiful summer afternoon in a Chicago suburb. He tells us he's a humanist, enjoys a facilitator's role mediating conflicts between marketers and researchers, and couldn't be happier. He reminds us of an early-aging professor of philosophy. Names and places have been changed.

We're a biotech firm that specializes in supplying the life science researchers worldwide with products that help them understand the processes related to working with DNA, RNA, and proteins. We've got a high degree of knowledge workers. High level of education. The corporation evolved because people followed things that interested them, just like organisms would focus on things that are of interest to them.

We have over 300 people here. Fifteen percent of the workforce have a PhD mostly in life sciences. Another 18 percent have a master's degree. Well over 60 percent have a bachelor's degree. And there are cross-functional groups that involve people from all different areas. It's a wonderful thing because we can be very responsive and give people opportunity, but it's also in some ways nebulous as to who you're reporting to and where you get this resource from and how you make sure you can control the work. People sometimes ask who's doing what.

We kind of joke about all these people who are so highly educated. There's also a lot of challenges with, "My way is the right way because I'm Dr. So and So."

Most of what we do is very much a team effort and we have a cooperative team approach to a lot of things. When teams don't work, I think there could be a couple of different elements. These might be polarized thoughts, but some teams don't work because you have too strong a personality either leading it or not leading it but sort of crushing everybody else's group consensus. They don't allow discussion. They don't allow resistance to ideas. They're just such a strong force of personality it maybe overwhelms the benefit you get from listening to other people. The other side is that you have teams that believe that total consensus is the only way to get anything done. I'm asked to help. "I'm having problems with this team. I don't know what it is. Can you just come and help facilitate some stuff?"

We've had discussions about, well, what does a decision mean? What does consensus mean? Some people say that it's absolute agreement from everyone that it's going to be done a certain way. Whereas my model is well, no, I think we should define consensus as can we all live with this decision. Yes, some of us have voiced our opinion. We disagree on certain elements of it. But what can we agree on and when can we say, "Yes, we'll do this"? It's part of the well of goodwill that you have to have in relationships where you always add to it. Some days you say, "I've got to pull from that well of goodwill now. And yes, I know there are big issues here." For some teams, it's who's responsible here, and a lot of times, people will abdicate their role responsibility by saying, "The team decided not to do it. I don't have to make a decision on that even though I know it's not the right thing to do."

You usually have to have several names on a patent application. But it's also interesting to hear people talk about: "Well, you know, his name got on the patent because he happened to be around." "I don't know why the (expletive deleted) his name's on the patent." "He's the kind of person who goes out and sucks in these kind of applications." There's a real sense of ownership of these ideas. And I think people are willing to share the ownership of those ideas with the people who helped them really formulate that process. There's also, I heard of two instances, when a person didn't do anything to get on this patent. They pulled a piece of it so they could put their name on it.

I've heard people say, "Well, I've got some good ideas but I'm not going to bring them forward yet. Somebody will steal them or nothing will happen with them."

In total, though, I think the spirit of cooperation here is pretty strong. People who can be good in some groups can be bad in others. Some get a reputation and nobody wants them. It's the island of lost scientists. The island of misfit toys. You can see them almost clustered together. They get assigned peripheral projects just because they're not working well with teams or they'll get minimized. And that's not a good thing to see. It's hard to get them back in the mainstream. Sometimes you can't resurrect them. Lazarus is there, but he's not getting up.

One thing, I'll go back to the sort of artisan mentality that exists. Scientists talk about "my hands." "My hands did this." And the reason they can't make it over in manufacturing is not because my protocol is not what it should be or I didn't get all the variation that might be happening in the process. It's because their hands aren't as good as mine. I spend a lot of time on those people issues. I always push the idea that the reason we're doing this is so that everybody will have a dialogue. And it's not just the conflict situation that you want to be zeroing in on, but what happens before the conflict situation and what happens afterward. I talk to people about conflict resolution skills. Well, a lot of that skill-set is based on what you do before and after. And how you build those links with people.

MEANINGS AND LESSONS

When scientists work together, they do some unexpected things, like remove the irritating team member from the group to "the island of lost scientists . . . misfit toys."

LESSON
If you think brainy people are more trusting and cooperative than common folk, read Emotional Intelligence *(8) for the truth of it.*

Strong personalities dominate some of their team meetings—my way or no way—a carryover from competition in graduate school. It reduces group creativity. But who claims anyone wants group creativity? If you listen to what Dean says about names on patents, you can see that the academic race is being carried on at work. The philosophical spin to the question of what constitutes consensus suggests that there is no

consensus. There is maneuvering for position and domi-
nance—that name on the patent.

Lesson
*If you want to learn how to really cut someone's throat, watch
the way scientists do it.*

Dean is perfect for his job. He's above the fray doing cerebral things for people who are cerebral in one sense only.
They are master technicians, good hands, in the most rarefied
way. In dealing with people, they are like everyone else.

I COULD PUNCH HIM IN THE NOSE

Eric is an engineering technician, a blue-collar worker in a
machine company. Eric's a "car guy" and from time to time he
drives his "batmobile," a black 1953 Olds convertible. His wife,
Ginnie, is a nursing assistant. They are outgoing, likable, hard-
working people, and good examples of the midwestern work
ethic.

ERIC: Bosses? Basically, but not always, most of my bosses were nice
guys. But you work with them also. And when you've been
around awhile, you learn how to tolerate people. Run them
around even if you don't like them.

Some people just aren't nice. You're a nice guy, but somebody down the road might not be a nice guy. That's the way
people are. They ask you to do something and it makes you
mad. Whereas a nice guy will ask you to do something, and
you're happy to do it for him.

It's just this one guy that I was involved with for the last 9
months or so that I just got rid of. He'd ask you to do something and right away you're ready to punch him in the nose.
His technique of handling people was so disagreeable to me
that every time he opened his mouth he made me mad.
Nobody in the place likes him. Right.

GINNIE: Some of the engineers are nice. And when you work with
them, you do everything to please them to get the job done.

If you work for someone and they demand it out of you, I feel that I am an adult. I'll work with someone, but I hate to say that this is the way you're going to do it and this is the only way to do something.

ERIC: This guy was supposed to coordinate all the activities on my job to make sure it was done right. So to do this, he would come and ask me what I'm doing and when I'm going to do this. And I would tell him, "I'm doing this today and it'll take me a day and a half. Then I've got to do this one here and then I've got to change this and do this." And he'd say, "Okay," and he'd walk away and write down everything. Then he'd come back with a schedule of what I'm supposed to do, and it was just what I told him I was going to do. I mean, it was a joke. He would never assert any authority with me because he didn't know enough about what I was supposed to do to tell me how to do it. So he'd ask me all the time, "What are you doing now?" And I'd tell him and he'd say, "Well, when are you going to do this?" And I'd tell him. And he'd say, "Okay, that makes sense." And that's the way he'd schedule it—the way I told him.

It doesn't make you happy. And that was why I was so frustrated with the guy and wanted to punch him in the nose and everything. And I went to the lab manager and asked him, "Why is this guy with me because we're not accomplishing anything? He never tells me anything. He asks me all the time. And if he's supposed to be my scheduler, how come he doesn't schedule anything?"

And all of a sudden, he wasn't bothering me anymore. So it worked. They got him away from me. Murph and the guys used to laugh at me when this guy was with me. And I used to say, "Please, Murph, take this guy back. Take this guy back." So now he's back with them, so I got the last laugh on them. He's not bothering me anymore; he's back bothering those guys.

You work with people so long. I never was going to let a supervisor drive me out of a job, because if the supervisor's not doing it right, they'll get rid of him eventually. I guess I could put out a contract on him, I suppose. [laughs] There's just ways of dealing with people. He took the credit for my telling him how to coordinate a job.

MEANINGS AND LESSONS

Eric's team that isn't a team was for a time dominated by a leader who wasn't a leader. There are no innuendos or subtleties on the shop floor of his company. A team scheduler who wasn't scheduling was as inappropriate as a crescent wrench would be when a hex wrench is called for.

How refreshing to hear about a no-nonsense blue-collar solution to a production problem. Very instructive is the comparison between Eric's story and Dean's in the preceding story. It's "hands-on" versus "heads-on." Let Eric stand for the directly traceable evolutionary line back to early "hands-on" such as sharp rocks, clubs, and toolmaking. Let Dean stand for the leap ahead into tomorrow involving knowledge workers with balloon-size heads. Their work represents different versions of reality: The Erics can see what they're doing, whereas the Deans infer it. Eric's god is older. Dean's is relatively recent in the history of humankind. What does this have to do with dumb bosses?

Knowledge workers put up with dumb bosses and make excuses for them more readily than hands-on workers. Knowledge industries tolerate dumb bosses longer than hands-on ones. Knowledge workers hide their true feelings, whereas hands-on workers can become uncouth and sometimes violent. These generalizations don't explain everything. No workplace is totally hands-on or heads-on, but the proportions of each may help explain some of the imponderable craziness you've been reading about.

The actual situation is more like this: Heads-on people rise to the top and lead combinations of hands-on and heads-on followers. A heads-on subleader, like the human resources manager in the story "The Morale Survey as Beauty Contest," works closely and identifies with the confusion of thousands of hands-on employees. Union members, in other words, may find release in a slugfest, but their more heads-on leaders know that picking up the stone and swinging the club will seldom solve things except as a last resort.

LESSON

You don't need a PhD to know how to get rid of a bad-actor team leader. In fact, it may help to not have one.

Eric puts his hands on machined components configured into a product. The drawings that define the product on a computer screen become a three-dimensional object capable of doing observable and immediate work. "Hands-on" is an honorable term that includes sculptors, artists, artisans of all kinds, as well as machinists, and mechanics. The "product," when it cooperates, is a "nice guy"; when it doesn't, it's a "jerk." Other people—coworkers and managers—are defined in the same way. Eric solves machine problems and people problems in a "hands-on" way: "punch him in the nose . . . Please, Murph, take this guy back."

Knowledge workers, as in Dean's company, live in a reality where "nice guy" and "jerk" mythologies to describe the world are not as potent. Instead, you see balloon-heads engaging in arm's-length manipulations, political trade-offs, and networking for tactical advantage—heads over hands.

One influence on craziness is that balloon-heads have a hard time imagining the feelings of stress, anxiety, and uncertainty in others. That blindness sets the stage for much of the dumbness in these stories.

LESSON

A heads-on manager won't know what you're talking about if you say you're upset. A hands-on manager will want to help.

We're sure the broader construction of these points has already occurred to you: Good counselors and therapists need a combination of both traits.

QUALITY:
SMART AND DUMB

Look carefully and you will see only two routes to quality: smart and dumb. Smart occurs when people trust their leaders, want to learn, and are proud of their product. Dumb is fraught with fear, lack of trust, and capped by poor leadership. We've said nothing about processes or machines because they are the same whether a company goes smart or dumb. Yet there are some combinations of person and machine which are worth noting:

1. A dumb (demotivated or untrained) person working on a smart (self-correcting) machine can produce junk.

2. A smart (inspired) person working on a dumb (error-prone) machine can produce gems.

3. A dumb person on a dumb machine always produces junk.

4. A smart person on a smart machine always produces gems.

Once you go beyond those alternatives, it gets complicated because the human component is so hard to control. Taylorism (time and motion studies) got close; industrial engineers still try, but the human spirit is unwilling to cooperate. Ruth, in Chapter Two, resented being treated like a robot, a perfect example. We all wish that statistical procedures and process could assure consistently high quality. But they can't. Current quality leaders explain:

It is a delusion that sound management can be replaced by an information format. It is like putting a Bible in every hotel room with the thought that the occupants will act according to its content. (Philip B. Crosby, President, Career IV, quoted in *Quality Digest,* April 1997)

ISO 9000 and ISO 14000 look a lot like the QA movement of the late 1940s. And what's new in the area of quality engineering? Our statistical methods look pretty much the same as they did in the days of Shewart and Fisher . . . One could even argue that we have failed to learn from our mistakes. (Thomas Pyzdek, President, Quality Publishing, quoted in *Quality Digest,* April 1997)

As an increasing number of companies are registered to the ISO 9001 and 9002 standards, the registration will be seen as a cost of doing business and not as a sign of quality. The registration as an indicator of quality will diminish. (Barry S. Herst, Director of the Office of Quality Programs NIST, quoted in *Quality Digest,* April 1997)

The efforts of millions of employees lie behind every product we use. If the item we purchase works as promised, we feel good. If it doesn't perform well, we feel cheated. Nobody says, "That product you like is the result of an international standard-setting, benchmarking system called ISO 9000." What?

Some of you will remember the name W. Edwards Deming (3)—no, not a foreign film director, but he could have been because his work had a human face—the American who almost single-handedly choreographed Japanese product quality beyond that of the United States. A hero too late in his own country. Deming's human face looks like you. It's your energy that powers trend lines on the graph hanging in the quality assurance office. But why care unless you are employed where every poster reminds you to "Think Quality"? You should care, though, because when a manager explaining those graphs doesn't understand whose energy it is coursing along those lines, he or she doesn't know what quality is and can end up destroying it.

Your Right to Quality

Let's speak about quality as it affects our lifestyle. Quality products and services, whether actually delivered or not, are regarded as a right of all citizens. Quality is practically an amendment to the Constitution. What began as a way to achieve a competitive edge has turned into an article of faith. Quality-mindedness is the American way, and we get upset when it isn't there.

Quality's transition from a plausible idea, to a necessary element in a competitive marketplace, to an organization's creed, to a national belief system is a fascinating evolution. People at the top have always been able to afford quality in everything. People on tight budgets have been made to feel they also deserve quality. However, return policies are being tightened by leading retailers because they cost too much. What that means is that a supposedly guaranteed right is being denied.

Quality's body of common law is set down in numerous publications of the American Society for Quality Assurance (ASQA). The U.S. Commerce Department's Baldrige Award Committee serves as a version of a quality Supreme Court, rendering judgments through prizes to industry's best and thereby defining criteria for workmanship. What they forget to tell you is that today's hero can be tomorrow's bum. Nevertheless, ignorance of quality standards is no longer an excuse. It's get smart, get quality, or get out of business.

Why then do we see managers smirk when their organizations introduce yet another "sure-to-work" quality program? Why do they say quietly, so few will overhear, "If people were only as smart as our (dumb) machines." Why is it that at every encounter with employees, team leaders, and managers, we hear stories totally opposite from what their companies are telling the press, business book writers, and their own employees?

What do the concepts of quality look like to the people who are right there where it's supposed to be happening? How do they describe the creation of their products? What do employees say when not in the training center and out of earshot of management?

Documenting Dysfunction Rather Than Quality

The paper trail of quality documentation is a barometer of corporate values if you know how to follow it. The values of the organization we're about to describe were revealed in two ways. One, of course, referred to product; the other referred to people. The product values were exemplary—to continuously improve quality, shorten delivery times, and pay attention to customer needs—straight A's. The values used in handling people were essentially straight D's, consisting of lack of trust, fear, and the threat of very hurtful rejection for transgressions of any kind as defined by autocratic leadership. Leadership, particularly its key managers, had smart product ideas but was dumb about people.

These are the parameters to keep in mind. Dumb leadership yields dumb, relatively useless information. Smart leadership gives worthwhile information. But how are quality assurance managers in dumb-functioning systems to know whether the computers are disgorging live or dead, smart or dumb, information? They can't, because they're trapped within a closed universe. The only way they might know is by understanding what the universe is really like. If the organization is dysfunctional, useless (dead, dumb, irrelevant) information will be processed. Who's to reveal the truth?

This niche-controlling company was growing profitably, establishing plants overseas, and continuing to pay well while increasing bonuses and benefits. So why should their 30 managers, with 20-plus years of experience on average, report confusion and fear? Why unhappiness and anger in times of plenty?

Merely a total change in roles, the imposition of self-directed team structures with its piles of required documentation—all without benefit of emotional and intellectual preparation. The owner just said, "Do it!" Three years into the "this-is-how-we-gotta-keep-up-with-the-latest-thinking" program, managers close to retirement were talking openly about "the day," bathroom graffiti was atrociously antimanagement, and supervisors were putting in 12-, 14-, and sometimes 16-hour days back-to-back. It was love/hate. How could it have happened?

In the understandable urge to grow and continue the domination of the niche it occupied, company leaders embraced what they perceived to be the format for the organization of the future. In doing so they pushed responsibility down the line to people who never bargained for it, many who never wanted it. It compelled adaptation to computer-controlled machines among specialists who manipulated tools with grease better than with keyboards. It insisted upon an empowerment culture for employees whose managers never experienced it themselves. It rained paper down on supervisors who were, for those purposes, word and number illiterate. And on top of that, it selected an ambitious, autocratic, fear-provoking young bull-of-the-woods as their leader.

A few managers, so frustrated and cynical about perception-twisting changes, when asked to name people they least trusted, listed the names of their top leaders. Some managers retreated from overwhelming responsibilities, abdicating their authority under the pretense of empowerment and harvested fear and low morale for management so desperate for the opposite.

Lesson

When you want to generate information about quality, you need a healthy, not a dysfunctional, organization.

Dysfunction can be the outcome of dumb (inept, misguided, insensitive, power-driven, unfeeling) leadership or dumb (tradition-bound, blind-sided, arrogant) organizational thinking. Often, both appear together as in the company just mentioned. We predict more and more of what this paradigm example shows as organizations, out of competitive anxiety, dash toward "technological fixes" without considering how the people who have to adapt to those "fixes" need to be helped to do so.

The story "They Prefer to Be Drones," in the following chapter, is about a workforce fighting to retain its identity by hanging on to an old, familiar technology. In that instance, as in the previous one, management makes the assumption that new technology is good, computers are good, and one must "go with the flow" of the information revolution. But, as we will see, certain facts do not support that kind of faith.

So, cry for the "stubborn" employees who are neither mean nor resistive and who keep their companies afloat in spite of everything. They know that computer-driven technology may not increase productivity and that lack of intelligence is not the problem. Such employees have the support of experts who write in the July 1997 issue of *Scientific American:* "For all the useful things computers do, they do not seem, on balance, to have made us much richer by enabling us to do more work, of increasing value, in less time. Compared with the big economic bangs delivered by water-, steam-, and electricity-powered machines, productivity growth in the information age has been a mere whimper."

The review article we're quoting, by W. Wayt Gibbs, is a well-documented piece which also evokes the pained humor of uncomfortable recognition. He says, "SBT Accounting Systems in San Rafael, California, found in a 6000-person survey that office workers futz with the machines an average of 5.1 hours—more than half a workday—each week. One-fifth of that time was wasted waiting for programs to run or for help to arrive. Double-checking printouts for accuracy and format ran a close second. Lots of time goes into rearranging disk files. And then there are games (recall Winston's story in Chapter One). All told, futzing costs American businesses on the order of $100 billion a year in lost productivity."

AFP—ANOTHER FINE PROGRAM

John is a manager in a globally famous auto industry company. He is a big, happy-looking, straight-speaking person, red faced with prematurely white hair. He attended our business school workshop about coping with change. He lived through the decline, rebirth, and still-current preeminence of his employer. Years ago, he told the group things were so bad that the famous product—like a mortally wounded warrior leaving a legacy from which myths are made—actually spoke to the engineers telling them how to change this, then that, how to reconfigure an assembly, change tolerances, use that kind of gasket, find better hoses. In other words, the dying product could, like something out of science fiction, outline instructions for saving its life. Those lifesaving procedures didn't require rocket science. An alert administrator with a decent reputation, able to obtain a line of credit, personal drive, and vision did it. That was then. Now, John explained, with time opening up and profits coming in, the company was getting serious (code word for self-important) about its visions, management philosophies, and quality programs. He hadn't meant to speak as long as he did. The woman from AT&T was nodding vigorously, her mouth parroting his words silently. The man from IBM smiled, then squirmed, smiled again, and finally laughed at the appropriate moment. The big man was saying, "So last week they gave us an AFP, another fine program."

His admission and complaint turned some people on and others off. The quiet engineer from Ameritech became a more active participant. The two administrators from a large company disappeared at the lunch break.

The message to the group was this: If one quality program appears not to be working, switch to another. There are

always others that appear on cue, almost miraculously, like desert wildflowers after the briefest of rainfalls. Every new program is a rebirth experience for management. Alas, the desert wildflowers droop, starved for water. The fine program takes the mind off the old one and is again replaced.

Employees who actually make the product or deliver the service soon become immune to the quality program procession. They do the right things independently of the programs, which exist in someone's mind perhaps half a continent away and on the pages of elegant reports employees never see. It's better that way for the company. Like lawyers arguing their cases before a judge, smart top managers seemingly live in a first-class world of procedure and ritual while their employees go about their tasks turning out product and delivering service.

MEANINGS AND LESSONS

Corporate leaders look at the night sky and marvel at its beautiful organization. They're supposed to look up. What hand did it and how can I bring such orderly constellations into my company? We don't blame them. Some think that way—except for those who read Stephen Jay Gould and Carl Sagan—hopeful that the next quality program surely will work and bring sweet order. It isn't possible, so say the world's religions, to literally bring heaven down to earth. Mythology can raise you up, out of your self, and if the quality god is in your soul, the product will be good. If not, no process transforms it. John was saying orderliness (quality) can't be imposed or imported down. Employees weren't troubled by lofty, nifty theories. If they were troubled, they'd never get to work, wondering what pose to adopt as the latest AFP came down the line.

LESSON:
One strong reason for good quality is that employees remain true to their knowledge and aren't panicked by fads and false prophets.

John did something for the members of the workshop that we couldn't do. He opened them up to themselves. John's version of Copland's "Fanfare for the Common Man" encouraged people to come clean about the pitfalls of their quality programs. We knew they weren't planning that, since talking about "change," the workshop topic, could be done at arm's-length and people could sound very smart. Pretense and looking good in the eyes of one's peers are common shortcomings of most workshops.

Why did the managers have to pretend about quality within their companies? That's a purposefully dumb-sounding question. Here we offer a special case example within the context of quality. The answer is that loyalty to one's company, in spite of everything negative that's been written, still exists among managers who are in the middle of the productivity effort. Of course they see mistakes and have been hurt by them. They have genuinely tried to make quality programs work. They have to because there is no one else. They've turned those programs over to self-directed teams and hope that telling employees they are empowered will carry the day. It's too risky. If they fail, everything goes down. So the managers pretend that quality is being created, to themselves, to the outside world, to their employees, and to their bosses. These men and women in positions of true authority are not kidding themselves. They are praying it will all come together and that the regularity of the night skies will—by some supreme act of faith—come down to earth, at least in their company. They aren't lying, nor are they telling the whole truth. But it takes a public confession to jar loose what they deny. Until they face the real truth about their programs, they are being dumbed down by the very culture they defend.

LESSON

Denying the weakness of your company's quality efforts will make you dumber, not smarter, and less fit for leadership.

LEADERSHIP BEGINS AT SCHOOL

The field of education begs to be analyzed through the prism of smart or dumb quality. We're with Ralph and Belinda, recently retired high school principal and grade school teacher from a small city in Massachusetts. Their middle-class city is a university town with a working-class section. They live in a large home with a high-vaulted living room ceiling, dark stained woods, replicas of antiquities such as are sold at the Metropolitan Museum of Art in New York City, big couches, bookcases—a learned-looking place. We liked the setting and we liked them. Ralph is a short, wiry man who keeps fit by taking brisk walks. Belinda is smaller and thin. He chooses his words carefully but occasionally gets carried away when his more assertive side takes over, as it does toward the end of the interview. She engages you with images, straight talk, and gestures like a tour guide. Names and places have been changed.

RALPH: We have our values upside down in the school system. And let me tell you what should be at the center of the school: art, music, and phys ed (physical education). Everything else is ancillary to those three. Let's go back to the Greek idea of a sound mind and a sound body. One reason that we're having problems is because our values are turned over.

Teacher burnout is a big problem! They come in on time, they stay in their classroom for the allotted amount of time, they leave on time. But what the children have accomplished during that day is very little. That's a description of burnout.

They've learned enough so that they can keep physical control of the classroom. But in terms of what the input is to the children, it's very little. And the teacher puts very little effort into the teaching during that day. Going into those classrooms to give them ideas and expecting them to follow through on those ideas are very difficult to observe.

In most cases, I do believe teachers go into the profession generally because they have a genuine interest in children and in what they are going to do to make the world a better place. But I think they've used everything that they know how to use and they're at a standstill.

BELINDA: I had a friend in lower elementary, Helen, the school psychologist, and she moved forward on relationships with teacher to teacher. Being more cordial to each other, more thoughtful, having no one left out. You get some of this atmosphere going and this reflects on the children. Things function well. But it has to come from the beginning. The beginning being saying thank you and how are you today, and consideration. Positive leadership. Positive leadership.

RALPH: As principal, my boss was the superintendent and he answered to the school board. I served under various superintendents. The good thing they did was to have an instant rapport. That's first and foremost with whomever they were meeting with, even a hostile audience. Connect with a hostile audience in a way that is positive. Change the minds and the perceptions.

I can remember that one man. He would come into a room and he could change the tenor of that meeting simply by being there. Not through threats, but rather because he had a unique way of presenting himself and his ideas in such a fashion that it wasn't perceived as a threat. People liked him personally. He was an excellent administrator. A good many meetings are negative, and with that leadership, that negative becomes a positive. But it's difficult to find that positive leadership. It's difficult to find somebody who can change the minds of other people.

I think you have to start from the bottom up, not from the top down. The bottom in this case would be the basic educational unit, which would be the elementary school. Motivational speakers are rare breeds. You need to have hands-on continuity.

MEANINGS AND LESSONS

Don't think you're hearing only about small-time things from a small-time couple. There are thousands of Ralphs and Belindas, who if asked would give the same spontaneous, nonrancorous, almost sorrowful, abridged story of lives in education.

Woven throughout their narrative are strands that explain the imperfect design of many of our organizations. Poor quality—what students take away from the experience—is the result. Ralph and Belinda say nothing about buildings, computers, libraries, transportation, neighborhood, how much they earned or wanted to earn. Those elements don't count compared with the underlying truth: Learning is mediated through people.

They speak resolutely, but to see them, you'd know they are resigned. They refer to the income gap, the poor kids, the lower fifth who are (to them) doomed. Ralph's prescription for a better system is blue sky.

LESSON

In schools and in business, leadership must speak both to employees (teachers) and customers (students). Otherwise, all you get is hopelessness.

Art, music, and physical education. The way they say it evokes an image of Greece in the fifth century B.C. with students in white gowns, playing, dancing, singing. They keep returning to that theme. They hold that image in memory, as if it will turn back urban warfare, where no one's poor and everyone's motivated. Ralph and Belinda are kindhearted people. They themselves are like the perfect children, naive and not too terribly touched by reality.

What Ralph said was correct: Start change at the bottom. We suggested peppering the system with leaders like his model superintendent.

LESSON

Quality is in the hands of the worker, the doer, whether tending a machine or teaching a group of students. Teachers get us closer to the action because the meaning of quality can be reduced to its primal form—to the one on one, to the "I do, you do, we do, you learn, or you don't learn."

SHOOT THE QUALITY MESSENGER

Jim felt pebbled ground beneath him. A chilly wind blew across his body. The sun was coming up and a cock crowed. It was a barren space dotted with tropical vegetation, and he began to shake. The minefield dream.

The phone rang and he awoke. Jim slept too late—those midnight movies—and again his wife had gone to work, leaving a note and coffee. The call answered his letter regarding a quality manager's job. They wanted to talk. "Sure, I'll come in at 11."

The dream proved to be premonitory—a minefield-type job. The setting is a technical college in the midwest. Jim is a quality professional who delivers information in a punchy fashion. We're at a corner table in a local coffee shop. There's a midafternoon lull. Names and places have been changed.

I can start with the technical college experience. First, coming to the college, they were interested in implementing a quality improvement process internally, as well as supplying the service externally to some of their clients. Internally is the more interesting story, though.

I entered an institution essentially that, 3 months prior to my coming there, the faculty had nearly taken a vote of no confidence in the administration. The union met prior to the contract being signed for the next year, and one of the items on the union agenda at the meeting was whether or not to pass a vote of no confidence in administration, which would have sent a message to the board and a lot of other people in the community.

I think the board suggested that the college needed to get into a process that would offer a platform for faculty and administrators to start venting some of the anger and distrust and other things being expressed all over the institution.

But I wasn't told that whole background in the interview process. I was employed because of that situation. That's how I see it in hindsight, given what I know now versus what I knew coming in the door. Nobody told me that there was a vote of no confidence and things like that. I thought philosophically it was a really good thing that the institution was trying to learn and implement the same things they were trying to teach to their customers. So I was really in tune with that but somewhat surprised by what I learned the first 90 days being employed there. Number one was about the vote of no confidence and how poor the relationships were at that point between faculty and administration.

I spent a lot of time listening during the first 90 days to faculty and trying to understand how it came to be this way. How did it come to be that you people don't talk to each other? And let me ask a very obvious question: Who are we here to serve? You know, in my mind, it was the students, and I saw this as a very detrimental relationship to that end. How can faculty and administration, who will only talk to each other through their lawyers, work cooperatively to provide the students with a quality education? How does that happen in an institution where relationships have gotten to this point? And I guess that's when I really started to realize what a huge undertaking this was going to be.

The accrediting association mandated us to come up with this plan, which happened very shortly after I was hired, and was also mandating that faculty and administration work cooperatively in the development of this plan. So we had two strong forces. One was being driven by the college maintaining their accreditation and one was driven by the board saying we want to see measurable progress toward this end. So there were some external forces really driving this change, and what we needed to do was create the structure. And it turned to be what we called this quality council, which was an unbalanced mix from a numbers standpoint of faculty, administration, and support staff, including janitors.

And I spent the first year in that institution really just listening to faculty rag administrators in this room. And really, frankly admiring administration for doing more listening than reacting, although I could see it was in their nature to almost fight back. But I do recall that faculty were dredging up things that had happened to them with past administrations. They had carried that baggage all the way along and just sort of invested those same experiences and characteristics in this current administration. And I think the administrators felt like, "Well, I'm not really responsible for all the things that have happened to you here and you're still attributing those experiences to us." The complaints were lack of respect, petty power plays within the institution, not granting what would seem to be reasonable requests.

We had a faculty member there that I thought was one of those people who was sort of the bridge. He was a person who was splitting his time between his contract which committed him to the classroom but also providing quality management training to businesses, which was unusual. And he had two or three children, and I remember an issue of insurance coming up where clearly the administration had some flexibility in granting this request. But administration was very hesitant to set a precedent by giving this person special consideration or any consideration at all. And I saw that as really petty because a lot was at stake.

He had a contract with one of our higher-profile clients, a city council. And he said, "You know I'm not asking for the world here. You won't even hear my request. I'm going to pull out of the contract. I don't really have to be doing this additional work that I agreed to do to help the college and to help myself, too, but I don't have to do it." And administration went to the wall on this, refused to hear his request for a variance on this healthcare issue for his children, and he did pull out on all of his contracts, creating quite a lot of embarrassment for the college.

They ended up throwing me into the situation to pick up the pieces with the city. I wonder if they fully realized all the costs of being so inflexible with this individual. And all the things that they suffered to their own credibility and reputation within the community over what I think was a small, small issue.

He said, "Forget it. They're never going to change." And his opinion carried a lot of weight with the other faculty members. I didn't know if it was something we could overcome.

The president was very much the power ideology leader. He was very interested in exercising his power and making sure you knew that he had the power to do certain things. And one of the games he used to play was calling you at 2 minutes to 5 to make sure you were still here at the institution. He would call and actually bring up a totally useless subject that we could have talked about the next day. And also, from talking to other administrators who he had done the same thing to, there was sort of this collective wisdom about why is he calling. And some were of the mind and backbone to say to that president, "I'm where I'm supposed to be." But it was so offensive. Or if he wouldn't catch her in, he would call the next day and say, "Where were you?" And she would say, "I'm where I'm supposed to be." And that would be it and she maintained that.

And so, if you had the backbone to stand up to him, I think he would accept that. He did it continuously and I think it was just to assert his authority. And I think there were better ways to do that, more enlightened leadership, as opposed to that top-down sort of, "I want to know where you are, what you're doing, every time of the day that you're supposed to be here."

I traveled 60 miles every day and my contract was coming up for renewal for the second year. It was right about the same time I was considering this other job and I started to think, well, you know, I've done this for a year. "Obviously, I've tried to work really hard here and do a lot of things that aren't necessarily the most palatable, to come in here and try to deal with the situation every day, and you've given me indications that you're happy with my performance," I said. "But you know, there are times when the weather is really bad. I'm seeing cars in the ditches on the way down. Is there any flexibility in this 8 to 5 thing?"

It was almost like because I was part of an educational institution used to starting classes at 8 A.M. on the button that administrators had to practice the same; we were in that same boat. And there was absolutely no flexibility. I was to be there at eight o'clock at my desk everyday, ready to work no matter what the weather. And in the back of my mind, the other opportunity began to look more and more attractive. I was very committed. And yet, that was one of the things that drove me away.

You figure at some point there's a bill coming due. Some consideration because of the amount that I've given. Then something comes up which wipes away all the good feeling. And of course, what do you end up with? You get angry, you get angry with yourself for having kidded yourself thinking someone's going to appreciate it, but that person may have left last year, and the new person doesn't give a damn.

It's easiest to treat everyone the same. But not everybody's the same. And you wonder how you can get to a point where you can find that balance between not having to manage the exception for everybody, yet still try to accommodate people's needs. Because everybody is so different. And I don't know that organizations are really succeeding in that regard. You know, the worst thing happened. I left. Which also caused the college embarrassment in the community.

MEANINGS AND LESSONS

The depth of relationship problems were hidden from Jim, so one wonders: Did the institution really want to employ him? It's questionable. Pressure was applied by the board and the accrediting association. Did some faculty and administration want communication to improve? Undoubtedly. Some few always stand for better relationships. As for the president, would a man who checks on professional staff to see if they are at their desks at 5 P.M. voluntarily embrace an organizationwide program that encourages trusting and empowered behavior?

The symbolism of the dream helps here. The president would prefer that Jim lay quietly in the minefield. Jim, awake, didn't realize the minefield still existed and moved to another location, although indications of danger were abundant. He assumed the terrain was safe, but it wasn't: He was lied to about the danger. Then he saw a colleague—the faculty member who asked for an insurance variance—blown away. When he requested his own version of a variance, flexibility in work-hours because of his travel distance, it was denied.

LESSON

Never expect the truth when you start a new job. The only question is how much are you being lied to, not if you are being lied to.

Jim's narrative is one of six that talk about educational systems. All the protagonists are brothers and sisters—too trusting and a little naive. Jim honestly thought he had a legitimate, not a window-dressing, job. Throughout his story, he continues to resell himself. Until in the end, he's personally hurt, becomes angry, and all the rationalizations come tumbling down. The man upon whom he hoped to rely said it, "Forget it. They're never going to change."

Embarrassing the college in the eyes of the community is mentioned more than once. It's a getting-even kind of statement—hurting back when you've been hurt—revealing the depth of misplaced trust and hope initially invested. Slapped around by the "powers that be," as Ken puts it in "Good Ideas from *Those* People?" is what Jim experienced. Being called on the phone near quitting time is what Ruth also experienced in the story, "Savage Management."

LESSON

Rule-bound leaders, in addition to provoking your anger, may be doing you a positive service uncovering your naiveté.

ACHTUNG ENGINEERS

Mention quality and most of us will think of cars. They cost a lot, are expensive to maintain, we love and hate them, but wouldn't be without one. Big and tall Andrew, a marketing vice president for a global electronics company, explains his version of quality. He travels throughout the world promoting new automotive products and lives in San Jose. We're in Berkeley, California, at a local diner. Names and places have been changed.

> I guess my observation is that when German engineers have a problem to solve, they begin to look for good technical solutions and begin to move those solutions forward. They don't worry about all of the political noise, either within the government bureaucracy or within the company bureaucracy or within their own hierarchy. If I say this, am I going to get promoted or am I not going to get promoted? Here's the problems that we have, and here are the various technologies and the various ways we can refine those technologies.
>
> They seem to stay very focused on their job and they also are seemingly able to better analyze some of these other conditions, relating them to the whole. Okay, it looks like there's a tendency for the government to make these changes. Okay, we'll consider that, but we're going keep things moving along. We're not going to wait for them to do that. We'll consider that, and it'll have some place, but here's how we're moving the solution along.
>
> My experience so far has been with BMW and Mercedes Benz as two independent German companies, but I've also found that there's a vast difference between dealing with the Opel engineers, Opel being owned by General Motors in Germany, and dealing with General Motors in the United States.
>
> But the Germans have a much better handle on it, and they're much more straightforward. They're more direct, and if something

doesn't work, they'll tell you it doesn't work. They won't beat around the bush. They're just much more into it and much more capable engineers. That's my opinion in this limited area I've been working in.

I think one of the things is that within Germany and within these companies, there are many more people that have technical backgrounds who are senior-level people. And so maybe they feel more comfortable working in those particular environments. Like reporting to like.

It seems, for example, in General Motors here, the way these older engineers have survived is they've made the right political decisions in their careers. And because there was such a glut of engineers, there's a big gap in the middle—there are young engineers and there are old engineers. And there's not a consistency or continuity of age, and so the old guys have become too much like political hacks. They've gotten the spoils from something, and I'm not sure that it's always been from good engineering.

Quality differences? Technology differences or something like that. If I had to bet my money now on some good technical capabilities, I would bet it on the Germans, one, and the Europeans, two.

Yes, teams are very prevalent in the automotive industry as far as teams go. I'd say incompetent groups are the current things that are in use in Japanese companies. Japanese management—incompetent groups.

It's no joke; it's a statement of reality. Because they're so groupish in seeking harmony. I wouldn't call it a team because it's just a group of people that get together and are working on the same problem. You might call it a team, but I'm calling it a group. A team to me has more defined roles. In other words, if I'm on a baseball team, somebody plays first base and somebody plays second base. But this is just kind of a group that is getting together. They discuss things in a group and they don't really have a good hierarchy for making decisions. In other words, my joke is you don't get a decision from a Japanese company because the janitor hasn't decided yet. And so the janitor hasn't joined the consensus. And part of the point of consensus is that people need to make decisions. Or have the experience to make decisions. Or have the background to make decisions.

So I guess what I'm talking about, what I'm saying, is I think that originally the idea in Japanese management of small groups getting together is a good way to convey information and it's a good way for them to feel part of the decision process, but it's not necessarily the best way to make the best decision for any particular given situation. So I think that the efficiency of group decision making has probably peaked out. That's one of the things that they're going to have to work on: How do you take this group idea and have them make better decisions? And do they make more formal decisions? Or how do they make more formal analyses of things?

It may be a little bit better here right now because in an American company, when you get a group together and it's not necessarily organized, there's usually one or two guys who try to be the leader. Because they're American. And that won't happen in Japan; they'll all be at the same level. And nobody will necessarily stand up to be the leader. The automotive companies are still working at refining the process and are really after continuous improvement of the process as well.

MEANINGS AND LESSONS

Quality and teamwork come together in Andrew's story, which is where they belong. He never says "quality," yet the inference is there in the homogeneous environment ("Like reporting to like") of German automotive manufacturers. The right teams exist by virtue of accepted common goals and a common language. Quality is the natural outcome.

LESSON
Teamwork is the father of quality. Separating those natural processes and imposing them are artificial and a cloddish exercise.

The Japanese, too, in Andrew's eyes, represent a homogenized approach to production, harmony, and consensus building. The janitor who has not yet voted captures it, even though a comic reduction of life. Continuous improvement is the result of unquestioning acceptance of "group-make" wedded to "group-think." The process obviously works and quality is the outcome. Andrew dismisses the team idea out of hand.

He raps General Motors for their discontinuity of engineering intelligence, the result of an earlier period of corporate dumbness. But he offers a profound clue for fixing American quality and team failure. It comes out of him spontaneously because he's a well-traveled, thoroughly American marketer. It's in the comments about Americans needing to take over team meetings. It is a wake-up call to management and reinforces what you've read about in "There Was No Real Team" and "Good Ideas from *Those* People?" Andrew doesn't make the connection, it isn't his job, so we will do it for him. Forget the self-directed perversion and let Americans be Americans of the best kind—taking charge with compassion.

MY BEST FRIEND DESTROYED ME

Her organization drained her heart, so of course her quality suffered. It was done politely—no hurry, make up your own mind—with the overlay of liberalism for which her TV station was noted. Lisa is an attractive African-American woman with a great deal of stage presence. She is an actress. She is introspective and quiet, then suddenly assertive in her presentation. We met late in the day at a Chicago restaurant. Names and places have been changed.

> I would say it was a good place to work because I was there 8 years. I enjoyed what I did. There were . . . I sensed that a number of people were very frustrated. They referred to the place as "golden handcuffs." I didn't think at times the people really cared very much about you. It was like whether the job was done or not. There wasn't that much concern about your growth or development as a worker. As long as the job was done, yeah, fine. Sure, go ahead. The salaries received were not very high. But supposedly, because we worked in a kind of collegiate, easygoing, casual setting, that was supposed to make up for it.
>
> I felt like there was no interest in my development and what I was bringing to the table. It was, "Did she complete her assignment? Did she do this? What kind of problems did you have and how much money should we give her?" Raises were like 2 to 3 percent, something like that.

I felt like they had people who didn't really have the experience and background to help you develop well as a producer. It was, "Well, we're putting this person in this position because you have to have a boss." They would say one thing and do another.

Because it was on a college campus, there were so many people who came to school there and stayed on because it was a great place to live and work. I think that some of the mind-set of the management basically was, "We're a good farm team for students" and "Find your niche as you see fit." People didn't leave there.

They put a person who had no real experience in television as our supervisor. She was selected because she had tenure. And we needed someone to keep track of the paperwork. But then this person tried to assert herself. The personnel in the department got very angry. That person was removed within a year.

Then they decided to end the program we were working on, and it had the highest ratings, and bring in a new department head. They brought in a person who decided to go in a different direction. My feeling was he wanted to do his own thing. My program tried to reflect what was going on in the community and tried to serve groups who had been underrepresented.

It's how I was treated when I worked on a program that wasn't successful. That program was overwhelming. I made a proposal of a program that had three parts. I was not given the resources or go-ahead as I wanted to do it. I chose a pretty ambitious topic and I got overwhelmed in the course of the production. I had other programs to do at the time. And I basically got afraid and fell behind in my scheduling. I had a couple of conflicts with my supervisor. So when evaluation time came, I felt that they basically were trying to destroy me. I thought it was done to demoralize me. I was not given credit for any of the positive things that I did. I acknowledged that myself, that, yes, I failed.

The person who was my supervisor had been my friend. It created some hard feelings between us two. It destroyed the friendship. It was a dynamic that I insisted was pervading the evaluation. That's why it made it so personal. The person was trying to get back at me. The evaluation was the turning point. It figured in my determination and decision to leave.

I have never used race as a reason for why things are done the way they were done or how people were behaving toward me. I guess I felt, even though I was the only particular person in that area,

I felt that I could handle whatever came my way. I think that race figured into it in terms of who I was culturally. My outlook and my style were very black, to the point, and I was always asked if I was from New York. My style was different. My perspective was different. My outlook was different. When I would conversely try to tone it down, I would be told, "Well, you're not assertive enough." I felt like I was constantly being put into a "trick bag." I felt like the rules were constantly changing. I felt they did not want me to have the best feeling about myself. I got good responses from the people I did work with. I was well thought of. I worked at making a name for myself. People did not like that. I had too high an opinion of myself.

I showed my friends the evaluation because I couldn't believe the way it was written. People disagreed very strongly. I also felt I had been there too long. I was frustrated and very unhappy with the social life. There was none for me. It was a very polite but relatively cold place. Other minorities felt that way. That town was like Disneyland. Then you realize you're with this group of people whose only experience has been, well, I grew up in a small town and I came to this town and stayed here because I had so much fun in college. I tried heroically for years. I tried too long.

MEANINGS AND LESSONS

In the end, it came down to Lisa feeling her identity was being taken apart, the "trick bag" reference. Once that began to happen, the squishy, laid-back social system, which had always been present, only increased her sense of vulnerability. That potent weapon of the powerful, the evaluation report, makes its appearance. It drives her crazy. This is not the first time you've heard how an evaluation report mashed the brains of an employee. Why so powerful? It's this. The assessment of performance comes from the one person above all others who can most affect the emotions of an employee, one's supervisor. That changes the meaning of everything. That document can alter reality: Good can become bad, up can become down, and smart can become dumb.

LESSON
Evaluations are a breath of the Old West. You're dead if you go up against a rigged jury and a hanging judge.

In the course of her narrative, Lisa is showing us a dumb culture in action. Self-indulgent, unfeeling, and lacking insight, that culture squashed her motivation, injured her self-esteem, and caused her to quit. When those four horsemen are in the saddle, forget quality. Staying too long on a job is no longer a surprising revelation. But staying too long because the work environment "was like Disneyland" is unusual. She was seduced and willing to wear those "golden handcuffs." Many were seduced, she says, some remaining forever, but can we blame them? Wonderment and excitement experienced in safety, like at a theme park, will still manufacture adrenalin, endorphins, and a high. That has to be worth something.

Growth is a word Lisa uses often and was dismayed to find the concept missing from actual supervisory practice. Deadlines and completions, a time-bound set of criteria (after all, it was broadcasting), comprised supervisory practice. Again, forget quality.

She couldn't make it work for herself. She claims she was too "real" for them, sometimes too aggressive, sometimes not aggressive enough. She denies race had anything to do with it.

There is fault on both sides—she doesn't deny she was failing—but the big story here is that her self-proclaimed "enlightened" organization permitted her to fail. Lisa's interpretation is they wanted her to fail and pushed her out.

LESSON
If you suddenly discover you're not wanted, it's not paranoia; it's a clear look at what was always there.

INTO THE QUALITY PARADOX

Here are the three voices of José, Lee, and Scotty performing a workplace minifugue. Compelled to sing within a confined range, they still produce acceptable music. The music they make working together is, of course, their employer's product. But how much more they might accomplish if the boundaries were expanded for them is anyone's guess. View these glimpses of life inside a metal fabricating company. Names and places have been changed.

José

My name is José. My English is not good. I'm a machine operator. I've worked here a little more than 20 years. The way a boss treats me depends on how open I am. Not all, but a lot. If I listen, I'm open to work. We have a lot of temps here. I don't feel like it's fair sometimes that they let them go early. It makes me worry, upset a little, and makes me think. They don't have no benefits. And always pay minimum wage. It's not fair for them. I'm not angry with the company. They have families. The company is getting bigger, but I can't talk about whether they can hire more permanent people. Sometimes foremen make me nervous. We used to have one who kept looking at his watch and looking at us, but he quit. Sometimes you have to look around for screws and washers.

One more thing I want to say. I'm happy. I say thank you God, I have a job. Also I pray for the owners too. I've been married for 28 years. I have four children and the youngest is 24.

Lee

I'm Lee. I'm a lead man supervisor here for 13 years. I'm in charge of 50 people. I have a manager. In my old job, the supervisor laid me off. It's a company where half are men and the other half are women. The supervisor liked this woman, but she and I had a real nice relationship as friends. If he saw me talking to that girl during break or working hours, he would get mad at me or he would yell at me because the girl had a good relationship with me and not with him.

I was doing a good job. But because of that, he was jealous of me and he fired me. He told me that he no longer needed my help. He said they were slow in production. But I didn't believe him. I knew why. We had plenty of work. I was tired of that job. They didn't give raises. They were always on top of people. You couldn't even go to the rest room, only at break. In an emergency, you would have to ask and they would keep an eye on you if you were there more than 5 minutes. Now they changed managers and they're more concerned with people. Now they get 5-cent and 10-cent raises. Now, if you're doing your work and minding your business, you're okay. Before it was like you were in prison. I felt I deserved better than that. I had a little bit of fear.

Scotty

My name is Scotty. How you doing? I've been here 16 years. I can remember when they were demanding a lot of overtime and they gave the temps the opportunity to work first. And I didn't like it too much. One time I came in and they took me in the office and said we can fire you for this. For coming in without authority. At the time, I felt it wasn't fair to not give me the opportunity to work overtime. They're saving money. They told me that seniority didn't mean anything as far as overtime. I'm the kind of guy that it takes pretty much a lot to get me pissed off. It made me like not to work as hard as I would normally work.

It just really hurt me when they said seniority didn't mean anything. They would have temps working 10 or 12 hours a day and I would only get to work 8. I didn't think it was fair. A few of us spoke up about it and they gradually changed. They started saying give the other guys first choice and then if they don't want to, grab the temp guys. They gave the lead person a list of everybody's pay bracket. And you would be last on the list if you were at the top of the pay bracket. I would come in at 6:30 A.M. and find some had come at 4:30 A.M.. The lead person's friends had been given overtime. It was bad for morale. I see a lot of guys who react by slowing down. I've never been in a fight.

MEANINGS AND LESSONS

Fairness. What's that? Consistent quality. What's that? Producing anything is accomplished through a series of trade-offs. José, Lee, and Scotty are resentful, but they want, need, and stay with their employer. All three have accommodated; they burn slow while the temp situation continues and enhances the profitability of the company. All report lethargic, we're-in-no-hurry positive change.

LESSON

Payback time seldom comes for the resentful employee. When the bills arrive, the rent is due, and the kids need clothes, you're happy to have a job. And your boss knows it.

Robert Reich, the former secretary of labor, would say that he could tell a lot about the companies he visited by talking to people on the plant floor. When they said "we," that was a healthy sign, but when they said "they," he knew things were not right.

Our three singers are describing "they" companies. The question to wrestle with is: Do "we" companies produce better quality than "they" companies? Who knows? There aren't many "we" companies, and the ones who were "we" in the past may now be "they." The "they" types, from time to time, can become "we" with a change in leadership. In other words, we should think in terms of quality cycles (companies are coping organisms) as we think of life cycles.

LESSON

If you can catch the quality wave, you can snare a good product or service, but no one knows how long that wave will last.

Is there a last word on quality? There is—a stretch perhaps—if you compare the quality movement with another worldview attempt to create better workplaces: the corporate health and fitness movement, whose roots are traced to the early 1940s with the Kaiser-Permanente Plan in San Francisco. Probably the best analysis of the corporate fitness premise is provided in Kenneth R. Pelletier's 1984 book, *Healthy People in Unhealthy Places* (19). The premise is that healthy people working in healthy places will be more productive, and it's true. Unfortunately, the initially enlightened route to health moved quickly from fitness programs (smoking cessation, diet control, alcohol reduction, exercise, etc.) into considerations of the cost of health maintenance itself. When it was discovered that helping employees stay healthy saved money, more and more corporations climbed on board.

The quality movement origins are about the same age as health and fitness, dating from Dr. Deming's work in Japan after World War II (3).

Parallels exist between the two movements. Both have spawned quasi-official infrastructures which give awards and regulate and establish guidelines. Both have created expert consultants to aid healthcare facilities or companies, as the case may be, to meet standards of acceptability. By whom? By the very people who develop regulations for hospitals and those who certify quality practices for organizations. Both have devolved into little more than a compulsive involvement with cutting paper dolls and exclaiming, "See how smart am I!"

HOW EMPOWERMENT BECAME A DIRTY WORD

Whoever it was that first introduced empowerment to American industry deserves to have a statue erected in their honor. Smelling a good idea, industry jumped aboard the empowerment train and rode it all the way to the bank. It was a concept easy to dress up smart, the date no one would be ashamed to bring to the party. And what a party. Banners at work proclaimed freedom from arbitrary management, increased personal responsibility, and respect for individual initiative. But after the band went home and the balloons fell to the floor, the tired dancers discovered that banners and balloons were, well, you know, words and hot air.

Individual initiative meant doing another person's job in addition to your own. Freedom from arbitrary management was as removed from reality as an ancient Egyptian glyph in the information age. Personal responsibility meant one washed one's hands before exiting the washroom.

We exaggerate. Some corporations are doing right by their employees and are confirmed in what they know to be good practice. But corporations looking for a quick remake found empowerment was a scent of heaven. Their training directors had learned broken-field running while trying to keep up with the fad of the month they were instructed to jump on.

Empowerment leads directly to another bestseller on management's Top 40: self-directed work teams. This approach to greater profits comes complete with its own language. Since language carries values, learn the language of self-directed work teams and you will know what it means. Its language sounds like a foreign tongue spoken fast the way Sid Caesar and Danny Kaye used to imitate foreign tongues in a missed-that-phrase-what-did-he-say gobbledygook.

What employees hear is a "word salad"—schizophrenic neologisms—composed of new age, visionary uplift, group dynamics and phrases from debunked earlier fads littering the road to God Bless Corporate America.

There's a serious flaw in what could be a very good idea. Empowerment in the hands of too many has become the justification for selfishness. Follow this encounter with a glum, not too glib group of training directors.

WE WANT YOUR TOOLS

Bob White had been telling us what a motivated, empowered group of training directors we could expect to meet. He had approached us at a book signing in a large midwestern city and asked if we would be interested in presenting a program to their local chapter of a national training organization. They usually get about 15 to 20 people. They couldn't pay but this was surely our market, so we said okay. It turned out the event drew about 60 people with 10 new members signing up.

Notices were sent out for a buffet dinner, business meeting, and then our presentation. They charged $18 for the evening and we were told the sponsors were very pleased. They grossed over $1000 less the hall and food, but couldn't cover our hotel, dinner, or gas.

We arrived early and found a lovely room, tall ceiling, nice furnishings, bright and airy. Our host, a man in his early fifties, arrived and was pleasant enough in spite of a very bad personal job situation. He was about to either get fired or have to quit. How happy can you be under such circumstances? We talked to him while people, over 90 percent of them women, arrived. Then we noticed something strange. No one came over to say hello to us or to our host. Well, we're in another culture, just not demonstrative, maybe thinking deeply, maybe not thinking at all. Maybe they're only empowered at work. It looked and felt bad.

Bob began pressing us to give a "demonstration." In other words, these totally ungiving people wanted us to skip the theory and give them tools. We weren't getting any warm, fuzzy, we're-all-in-the-family feeling. Well, we thought, who are these angry-looking people calling themselves professionals urging us (through Bob) to give them only what they want, not what we spent days preparing?

The meeting began. The usual boring business. Then, an energetic woman jumped up to excitedly tell the group that their true guru was coming. He was going to teach them "to dialogue." "His" event would need some help since it was going to be BIG. Airport pickup, hotel, the whole 9 yards. Wow, were we impressed, waiting to go on. Was it the coming of the man or the coming of the dialogue? We felt they certainly needed dialoguing.

Our segment finally began with a very, very short introduction, read from our book. Monotone, no friendliness or creativity. When did we lose Bob as a friend? Fun and games time. No smiling faces. Arms folded into chests. Can we take an hour of this? We were prepared with table games, a trainer's delight and on a par with icebreakers, and a rundown on current books offering training solutions, selections from management bibles. Theory and deep thinking were what they were getting. They were turning more and more dour. We gave them a task to do at their tables: create a solution to the ills of training today. That consumed about 25 minutes as their round tables buzzed. The men (all five together at one table) were easy to track—they liked it. The women were forced to work together—an iffy deal. Each table picked a chairperson, and that person presented the group's findings.

Things never got lighter, and we were anxious to leave. A man from a local bookstore brought about 100 books, some were ours, none of which were sold that night. We saw empowerment in action. Bob White said, "I told you. You should put on a demonstration!"

MEANINGS AND LESSONS

There's a message here. Liken a trainer to an auto mechanic working off someone else's material, a training manual. The manual can be great, good, or mediocre, and so can a trainer. That's the way it works. Here's how it should work.

There was a German-trained Mercedes Benz mechanic, Albrecht, whose shop was in an out-of-the-way small town in Wisconsin. Albrecht hated the designation "mechanic" and we agreed. When you arrived for service, he would suit-up like a surgeon, rubber gloves and all, before he opened up your car's hood. Everything was spotless. His partner, also German-trained, was a younger English woman. Their shop was better organized than the offices of many physicians, accountants, and lawyers. Their work was like poetry put to music—precision movement, gleaming surfaces. We would watch transfigured. When the old Benz left his shop, you felt as though you yourself had been given a new body. Of how many trainers can you say the same?

LESSON

Most trainers, like most auto mechanics, are mediocre, and it doesn't matter how good their manuals are.

Another suggestion. Is there really a need for a "training department"? Training rightly belongs in the hands of those who must rely upon the performance of people who need new skills to do their jobs. "Every Manager and Supervisor a Trainer" should be the motto of an organization. What's the point of farming it out when it can be kept where the action is? Not only will you be saving unnecessary overhead, you'll be setting the stage for managers to learn a teaching skill previously denied them because of a silly tradition. Put the good manuals in the hands of good managers and you'll see how fast people will want to learn.

LESSON

Think about training as you would a just-in-time component. Deliver it when it's needed by the people who rely upon it to do their job.

Our comments about training received confirmation in *Industry Week*, January 5, 1998. The magazine summarizes the results of a 2-year landmark research study of how 1000 employees at global corporations learn. Sixty-two percent of what's needed is learned at the job site. "The core finding . . . will send shivers up the spines of corporate America, which spends $56 billion annually on formal training programs," the report said, and added "there must be a culture of openness and trust that is more than empty words."

WE NEED YOUR IDEAS AND EXPERIENCE

This story is the contrasting experience. It's where we heard the insider's view concerning empowerment and self-directed work teams. This other-side-of-the-coin event raised troubling questions for us. We were at a huge electronics trade show and convention held once a year and attended by engineers, production and quality managers, CEOs, CFOs, and COOs. The half-day workshop we presented, "Introduction to Team Building," was attended by 15 men and women whose multi-national electronics companies paid $595 each to participate. These 15 people ran large plants in the United States, Canada, and Puerto Rico. Their average age was about 40, they had been around, couldn't be conned by slogans, and the team concept wasn't getting them anywhere. What was wrong or right, they wanted to know and could we help?

The mood of the workshop was high discourse, word-plays, group laughs, and easy storytelling about their company's culture, product mix, failures, aspirations, and networking. These were loyal, brave, and generous men and women who knew that empowerment (they believed in it philosophically) was a sham and that self-directed teams seemed almost to go against the natural order of things, at least where they worked.

Within the larger workshop format, we presented two smaller self-contained sessions about trust and participation. The group completed self-revealing questionnaires, talked about what the results meant, and created impromptu scenarios illustrating the upside and downside of trust and participation in the workplace. We talked theory, talked and talked, they performed, and laughed at each other's stand-up comic descriptions of mistakes during a now frenzied, now calm, now provocative 3+ hours. It was, they said, the best workshop they had ever attended, and their evaluation sheets confirmed it.

What had happened compared to the training director group? It wasn't what we did or didn't do in a structured sense. The difference was in the nature of the groups themselves.

Managers live in the midst of bombardments of demands, schedule changes, switches in production runs, policies, and priorities, and are part of the blood and pain occasioned by those elements; trainers hear the bombardment and only read about the blood and pain. Managers live or die on the basis of real outcomes; trainers live and die on the basis of rating scales obtained far from the field of battle. A manager's vision is built upon immediate experience; a trainer's vision is of videos and seminars. Finally, managers are indispensable; trainers are dispensable.

Lesson
When your on-the-spot managers say self-directed work teams aren't working, believe them. Sending in the trainers is an affront to your managers and demeans your employees.

THEY PREFER TO BE DRONES

There is a vampire loose in Marc's company, draining the blood of old and loyal employees unable to defend themselves. They come to work in fear and return home so weakened by the struggle to master a new technology that when they hear the flapping of wings they succumb and can do nothing. Marc has been offering them the equivalent of a cross and garlic, but to obtain it they must have faith and trust the new technology enough to renounce the old. Most refuse. It's evening, and we're in a noisy, popular diner in Des Moines. None of us sees the vampire's shadow on the window.

Marc is a 42-year-old production manager employed at a book publishing company that's been in the same family for three generations. He says some of the patrons work at the university and for white-collar companies like his. Marc is married, a happy-looking man, round-faced, with black curly hair and dressed in a suit. He has a booming voice. His wife is employed. They own their home and have three grade school children. Everyone is multitasking their lives, and so there is chronic pressure and stress. Marc is introspective, bright, and likes dialogue. He's a good example of a baby boomer manager who works hard, sees, and is caught up in corporate contradictions. He doesn't see the vampire looking at him from the other side of the window, but he knows his employees look scared white, are giving up, and can't understand why. Names and places have been changed.

We're a book manufacturer. We do the prepress, press, web presses, binding, the complete job, finishing and making books. There are 600+ employees, 80 million annual sales, in business 100+ years. We're family owned, same family, third generation, never had layoffs. People are very comfortable about being taken care of. It's still a family-value type company, probably with some of the best benefits and leave time. It's nonunion, which has helped the change process. Our employees have a very strong voice about what they like and don't like to do.

The average age is 47, and those with 20+ years of service we're probably talking somewhere in the 300 category. There are people who retire with 60 years of service. Think about that.

I'm involved in implementing a computerized scheduling process. We bought new technology without any systems or education in place. So what we're doing is tearing down our old system, which people are very comfortable with, and bringing up a new system but without any support in the organization for any of the new systems.

I think all of us feel they'd be pretty comfortable if they didn't have to change. We have gone from a craftsmanship world, where you could hide behind the process, to a very visible technology. It's a change from a craftsmanship mentality to a technocrat mentality. I have to know how to manage a technological process versus a craft process. Which kind of means to people, "I can do stuff to get the results I want but could never explain it to anyone."

There's an analogy to this in the mid-1950s when we went from sheet-fed to the web-press technology. To go from sheets to the web was a technological leap for the company. And there were those who didn't believe that you could get the same type of quality.

What happened there was one machine was bought. The owner was the champion for learning this process. He was actively involved in actually running and learning it and passing that on to other people. Today, as we go through this next evolution of change, it's like the digital age. You don't have a champion learning it first. You have the people who have to learn the new craft trying to be the champions for it.

It's the customer who drives that decision for us. "Everybody else is doing it. How come you don't?" So we take a reactive approach to some of this technology, and I think it's probably a smart decision when you can look at it in the rearview mirror because when you do that you at least assure yourself that whatever you're getting into is now a proven technology and you don't spend your resources going down the wrong path. This is something that's stable now in the industry and no longer an alpha or beta site.

Sure we lost business, and that's why we're changing now. Because we're starting to see that other customers are saying, "The guy up the street can do this. We're going to give him the business." I'm always rooting for the customer. He's our champion for change.

I ask myself how much of a technological leap a human can make in a lifetime. I don't know the answer. As someone who's skilled and learned in technology, I am comfortable. Those who don't have the core competency, though, I don't know how they can possibly grasp new technology because it's a leap. Part of the game is I have to learn and run and be profitable. And how much time do I give myself or my organization or others?

We have this issue, it's this ability of someone to let go of a process they are very comfortable with and have control of. I think that's a big issue. But now they know they did something, they got feedback about it, and this feedback was paper—paper-based. Now it goes into a system and they *think* they did it. There are ways to find out if they did it right, but they're not going to check themselves.

They do want to be drones. I think you brought up an interesting point about drones. You know, a lot of management science has suggested an empowerment myth. I meet parents who have children the same age as ours and we talk about our careers and time and family values keep pulling on us—on the next evolution of change, which is saying you may have to sacrifice something for it. But have people decided that there was something more important than the change process, which is mainly their children? Somewhere along in my life, my parents had to decide, "I've got to take care of my family," and that's what they did. And that meant you went and worked for someone. And they took care of you and that took care of your family.

Today's models challenge all of us because I've got to take care of myself, and if I do that, that might mean I have to learn so much more than has ever been required before. Yet, how do I keep my family value intact because it's tugging on the time I have with my family? And I don't know if people have been misled on that premise about how much time are you supposed to spend with your family. And how much time am I supposed to spend on my development, which is being rapidly challenged because of technological change?

It's not that I don't want to be with my family as much as I just always feel a sense of urgency based on obsolescence. I have incorporated that into my mind-set. Now it may be a lie. In fact, I was thinking as I was driving over here that one of the comments I wanted to be sure to share, because I think I was lied to once, was the sex-drug-rock-'n'-roll theme that was prevalent when I grew up as an adolescent. And now am I being lied to about what the technological theme is, which is keeping a sense of urgency so that you're not obsolete. But is it a lie? I do have a family and I want to be with them, but I'm also feeling the sense of urgency. I have to know the technology better than anyone else. But as I go on further and as I sit back and reflect, maybe I've been lied to. Maybe I don't need to do all that. We weren't supposed to trust people over 30, but now we're all over 30, so I can't claim that one anymore.

How do you use technology to keep things simple still? And I think the natural tendency for anyone who's technology-driven is they don't want to keep it simple. They want to add the complexity because they feel they have to use it. It's there, so I must have to use it. I have to throw the kitchen sink in because I can, not because it makes sense. Not because it's something we can deal with. And I think that part is real important in implementing any of these technologies. It's being able to take those small steps and continue to learn versus throwing the kitchen sink in and then making it so complex that nobody can figure it out and then making people obsolete.

The clock punching mentality. How do you get your work done plus learn? And we also have the other values which are coming in there, which is comp time. This extra time can be used and taken off without question, but some of us feel that that comp time is really a false bank account because I'll never collect it. I'll never take advantage of it.

If we had a good master plan that had some integration back into the organization, some kind of alignment back into the organization, I think that would help solve things. One of the things that is always a challenge for me is to go back and visit with management and say, "What do you want me to do? We can't make the leap. This person's washing out, so what do we do with this person? We're trying to figure out what to do with this person. It's a resource that I have but I have to find a way to make them a success. It's very difficult for me because I could find the easy out, but let me hire some better resources." But their response back to me as a manager of a department is, "Develop those people." Now, how do I shake your foundations and put some sense of urgency that while you have time to get on the train, how long do you think you have? Management has told me, "Here are the handcuffs. Develop them. Your job is to make them keep raising the bar themselves and help them jump, leap over."

I'm the bad guy with not a lot of support from the top. The golden rule is silence. Not stopping the process, but giving us enough rope to hang ourselves. And you have to relish the role of taking the risk. You have to take that risk for small steps, which means we get burned but it didn't cost us the family farm. It was a mistake and it cost us something, but it's nothing anybody will measure and come back and say that cost us $500 or $10,000 or $100,000. It's known but there's the confidence that while we've made this change, these changes are so minuscule most people don't know it. We're seeing the effects and then hopefully can scramble back. And that's the strategy that has been very difficult to adapt to because you would like to have a whole systems approach to the integration of the project. In fact, this project is probably more of leading the change throughout the whole organization than the actual product it's supposed to develop, which are schedules. It's actually being used to help identify operationally all sorts of areas which need attention.

I think what's happened is we're implementing technology that's not IS (information systems) friendly; it's not people friendly. So there's such tremendous resistance. And that doesn't have to be in today's world. You can buy software products that are very user friendly. It empowers people to get and maintain the state of the art easier than we do, but we have a 1970s technology that we struggle with.

The emperor has no clothes. Someone made a decision in this privately held company; an owner made a decision and the easiest thing for all of us to do in this next layer of management is to hide behind something that was said a year ago, 5 years ago, 10 years ago, 20 years ago. So and so said, and that's why we're doing it that way. Instead of challenging what so and so said. Now that they're no longer part of the active process, they should challenge it even more. But it's very hard to challenge that because now I have to take a risk that I'm supposed to know what I'm talking about. And if I'm in a company where I haven't made many of those decisions, those risks are high-profile risks. But those values belong to people who are no longer there except in spirit. It's like fighting a ghost.

It's not being willing to take a risk over what the grand Poo Ba said. Even though you probably know in your heart you're right. That risk is high-profile lose, but low-profile win. The legacy of tradition, that's how we succeeded and that's how we'll remain. Even though it doesn't make any more sense in today's environment. And people hide behind it or are comfortable with that because now it's similar to doing skunk work. We're here to stink it up more than we think it really is for the results that we're supposed to get. Which may be true.

There's something about chaos that's important in an organization. It doesn't help motivate change. It's very easy to talk about the sky falling and it's easy to hide in chaos.

MEANINGS AND LESSONS

Marc's story is about the fear of change and about unseen, supernatural forces that can turn employees into zombies (drones). He's describing a technological upheaval as powerful as a storm that can alter the land it passes over. It's all that, plus one man's visit into himself.

Like prophets of every age, Marc is looking for meaning in a chaotic world. He has embarked upon a path that will require a new language, one able to define the changing reality. Somewhat like a Moses of technology, he must reassure his employees that their journey will be a safe one. He asks, but gets no help from "on high." He's "handcuffed," he says, and feels alone in what he portrays as a twentieth-century desert.

People who work for a living are supposed to know what the words *change* and *fear* mean, but until you are part of it and are able to talk about it, as Marc did with us, change and fear are just words. They are words which imply that employees all share a common experience, the challenge of mastery, to make it happen, embrace it, and learn from it. Marc wonders what words and actions might create such personal transformations. He says his employees don't want to learn. They like the world the way it is, being in control of publishing processes they can see and manage.

Marc talks about his ambivalence, hanging on to the old, assessing the new, and caving in only under the threat of lost business. He loves the customers. When he talks about "skill sets," the phrase is devoid of feeling and he sounds like a consultant. It's when he personalizes the story, referring to values, to his parents, to his wife and children, to the school system, that Marc becomes a middle manager speaking for millions like himself.

LESSON
The ambivalence that accompanies today's technological revolution is seen in the stories people tell, not in the glitzy hype of business magazines.

We're listening to an upwardly mobile, bright, motivated man who finds himself—13 years into his job—a well-paid victim of corporate uncertainty. He knows he is party to that uncertainty and only now is seeing the negative consequences. Without realizing it, he has become the vampire's helper. Marc can't convince his employees that they will be in no danger by following him into the dark passages.

Marc is showing us those dark passages which lead from one world to another. He's a twentieth-century voyager—little different from those of the fifteenth century—setting forth from a place of predictability toward the uncertainties of a mist-shrouded, poorly defined horizon. He's recounting the inner life of all voyagers—questioning the values underlying the transition between one level of technology to the next, doubting his perceptions, challenging supreme authority and getting no answer—while on the surface urging his employees to risk everything on a promise of safety which his own god (the "Poo Ba") does not openly support.

As he evokes the image of the generation that couldn't trust anyone over the age of 30, horrified by the knowledge that it has all come full circle, he is reciting the unspoken mantra of today's typical managers: "I want to be the agent of peaceful change. I am not a destroyer. I want to be the agent of peaceful change."

LESSON

To lead positive organizational change, managers must instill trust among employees before taking them through the frightening world of the newer technologies.

THOSE LOONY MEMOS COVER MY WALLS

Connie has taken her mean dean's loony memos and stuck pins in them where they hang lifeless on her wall. It's her version of voodoo—she wouldn't admit to that, but we are in a New Orleans parish—where pins stuck into an artifact taken from someone you want to hurt are claimed to work. She would deny such a belief. On the other hand, she's writing a murder mystery set on a college campus.

Connie's a professor of humanities in a community college of 10,000 students. She's been there for more than 20 years. We were invited into her neat, well-arranged home outside New Orleans. There are dabs of original art, a hot tub on an enclosed porch, piles of books and magazines, and an old brown cat that hides under her covers from strangers. It's a pleasant setting for a discussion about what's wrong with our colleges. She's a generous person who loves teaching in spite of an administration that seems out to destroy the motivation of its faculty. Places and names have been changed.

This dean chewed me out for being sick. She had come up with this policy but hadn't announced it yet. And I'm the kind of person that goes in with the flu. When I had my surgery, I refused to let anyone else grade my papers. I was recovering from surgery, sitting on this porch, grading papers like mad; that's the kind of person I am. I was the worst person to do that to. She had really picked on absolutely the wrong person. I'm the one that everyone says is conscientious to a fault. To a fault. She chewed me out privately. But it hurt me. I was so stunned I didn't know quite what to say. Then when I saw her in the hall, I looked her right in the eye and smiled. I felt at the time that I had never been spoken to like that by a supervisor in my whole life. And remember she was a student of mine once, too. It made me feel like, oh (expletive deleted).

I have a friend who says, "No good deed goes unpunished." [laughs] I'm not a vengeful person. I was quite surprised by it because I thought I had a really good relationship with her, but since then I've found out that nearly everyone in the department has had a similar experience. "Yeah, she did that to me, too." Everybody's getting a little concerned about her and wondering if something's going on.

It has made me less interested in volunteering for things. I was always a volunteer. Now I've been taking all of her memos and every one of these loony memos that keep coming out. You must get the dean's permission. I've pinned them all up on the wall, and anytime I'm asked to do something extra, I force myself to sit for a moment and read every one of those memos before I decide.

It's not a real highly paid profession for the amount of graduate work and so forth required to do it. But there are the benefits you don't get in other professions. There's also the fun of teaching.

It's interesting because we're just about to face our reaccreditation process, which we have to do every 10 years. The people come in and decide if your degrees are worth anything. They examine every facet of the college. Personnel, policies. One of the requirements is that faculty be involved in decisions concerning the college and that everything be in the process, that the entire community college be involved in decision making. That's a standard you have to meet. Most of the faculty do not believe that particular criterion is being met.

There are decisions made at the top without consulting the faculty that directly affect the faculty. For example, there are decisions concerning the library. The administration, in 1991, decided we would not buy books. This was done without consulting the faculty. Their feeling is that everything should go electronic and Internet and CD-ROM. It's fine to have those things, but these people don't seem to understand that you also need books.

We used to have a library committee, but it was disbanded. It was just announced one day. There are a lot of things done by fiat. Another one is deciding there's going to be a computer lab set up and not consulting faculty about what they need or want. They just did it over the summer. We came back and there was a computer lab. Some of it was useful and some of it wasn't.

We have newsletters. Sometimes we are asked to give input and even to vote on something and then it's completely ignored anyway. Just simple things like whether to keep the tree outside the college. Everybody said to leave the tree and they chopped it down.

Ever since the new administration came in, more and more this is the way it's gone. The union membership continues to grow in spite of the fact they've hired very few full-time faculty for the last 5 years. It's less expensive. They're way overloading their middle management, like the dean. My dean formerly handled three divisions and now she's dean of all of them. Plus she has other responsibilities in addition to that. That affects us.

In the olden days, they would have a search committee. Now, the supervisor of that administrator hires the one they want. A few have come from the faculty. Most of them come in from the outside. The board of trustees hires the president. He hires everybody else. When the new president came in, we had several Friday night massacres. People would be told not to come back on Monday, and then he brings in his own people. The president has to have a doctorate, experience, and so on. He has a free hand. The district provost is the real boss. The president is never there. He's a golfer. He shows up for graduation. I was used to a president that had an open door, even if only. "Hi, how are you?" A couple of times, I called and was told, "We'll call you back when we find out when he might be available." And it might be next week.

It is all negative, but not on my performance. Some feel nobody cares, so they're not going to put themselves out. Some people get very discouraged, and working 60 hours a week isn't going to do them any good, and no one rewards them for it, so they don't do it.

I feel I'm a professional. My responsibility is to my students and me. I wouldn't say a majority of my colleagues feel that way, but a few do. It doesn't matter which subject they teach. Your profession is teaching. I'm constantly amazed at the outstanding jobs that most people do for so little in the way of a pat on the back or anything. You get your feedback from your students.

One of the problems of education is that the good teacher will teach well and the bad teacher will complain. And if that's so, it gives license to some administrators to screw off and some do. In education, the experts about teaching are the teachers, not the administrators. In higher education, you will find that the administrators are not people who have come out of the teaching field. They've come out of the education administrative classes and they're theorists. They can have lots of great theories, but when it comes to motivating those kids to do it, it's a very different kind of thing.

Somebody's got to sweep the floor, pay the bills, order the toilet paper, make sure we get the money to run things. My experience with most administrators, not all of them, is that most of them don't like academic people. Don't like and respect academic people. That's why they went into administration. That way, they wouldn't have to be in the classroom. It's a funny thing, but those people don't want to be in the classroom. Step into my shoes. It would solve a lot of problems. A lot of them have very narrow educations. They may go into it because that way they don't have to take a language or humanities. A lot have doctorates in educational administration, which I think is very narrow. They have a DEd, that's at the community college. At the university, you would find that more of them have degrees in physics or chemistry or whatever.

My dean has a doctorate in English. She happens to have been an English teacher. She is an exception. She has the credentials. When she crossed over the line, she became part of a different culture. I happen to have known her since she was a student of mine when I first started teaching. Without a search committee or anything, it was suddenly announced—and she had no administrative experience, had never been a chair or anything—it was just announced she was going to be dean. The president appointed her. She was his personal friend. She helped him write a book. Sex was not involved. It was quite a surprise; people were talking about who should apply. Nobody even thought of her. She's a very quiet, reclusive person, never been on any committees, never took part in—and suddenly, bam!—she was dean, just like that. There was significantly more money.

I still think that I would rather be, salarywise and job security-wise, on the faculty than in administration. A lot of faculty feel that way. Sometimes you're better off not being promoted. They keep piling more responsibility on her and she's getting more and more remote from us. Therefore, she's becoming stricter and stricter and trying to micromanage more and more instead of delegating and giving up things. I think eventually she's going to explode. She does everything herself.

The previous dean gave a lot more responsibility to the chairs to do the scheduling, evaluating. She doesn't let the chairs do anything like that. She's done some things very well. There are things that are pretty peculiar in a college situation. Like you have to ask permission to cancel a class from her directly. If you're sick, you have to call her at home to get permission to cancel a class. We used to just tell the secretary, "I won't be there; put up a sign." Then you'd tell the dean later what the problem was.

But no matter how bad things get like that, I always know I can go in my class and shut the door and then it's gone. It's just gone. Nothing else really matters when you're in that room. Really, there isn't any other universe at the moment except that one. You have to concentrate so hard. All your nerve endings come to the surface. You're on stage.

MEANINGS AND LESSONS

Sticking pins in her dean's memos is Connie's way of ensuring her survival and handling her stress. She remains smart through her love of teaching. Her administration remains dumb because they're spreading fear and resentment among faculty.

The dumbness of this story writes itself. We're looking into a bureaucracy through the eyes of a dedicated, long-time professor who will teach well no matter what. Connie keeps getting smarter because her nerve endings are stimulated in the classroom and she's writing a novel. She's part of life, she's good, she feels it, and knows it. The administrators can't feel anything—no more books, micromanagement, overloading middle managers. Let's play golf. Why bother with books when you can read anything you want on the Internet. Just click on the teacher's face.

Dumb administrators make a mediocre faculty even dumber. Students suffer because of dumbed-down teachers. The same is true of dumb bosses—employees stop learning.

Connie's dumb administration starts back with the board of trustees, local businesspeople, who apparently selected a self-indulgent fool for a president. He's a fool because he doesn't know what's happening at his community college and should or he does know and doesn't care. The provost's dumbness is even worse. His management style directly affects faculty and students. It was he who transformed a perfectly acceptable English teacher into a compulsive memo-writing dumb dean. If she does explode, something that's possible according to Connie, her internal yet-to-be-written memos could splatter her office walls. Finally, publishing newsletters promoting empowerment while denying it in practice is something dumb organizations always do. It's always a good barometer of what's really going on.

LESSON
You can't run a world-class company with leaders who don't like employees and don't care whether or not they are still learning, anymore than you can run a world-class educational system with administrators who don't like teachers or teaching.

The vote of no vote along with the meeting of no meeting are other parts of Connie's life. These are typical occurrences among autocratically driven organizations. All organizations can purchase books and training videos about empowerment while at the same time calling "no" meetings and holding "no" votes.

OUR UNIVERSITY IS A DYSFUNCTIONAL FAMILY

We're talking with Bonnie, a midlevel administrator in a large midwestern university system. She's an outspoken—some would say brash—woman in her early fifties, an animated "you want a fight, I'll give you a fight" kind of person who's been in her job for about 20 years. She was more than happy to discuss her university system and university systems in general. This part of the interview focuses on the question of empowerment.

[makes face] Overall I think the type of people who work at the university would not lean toward helping anybody. I think they protect their turf. They're centered in some way. I think they get into a box. I think that, to me, the university is right next to working for the government. They're in business for themselves: They're not employed by you, they're not employed by me, they're not in private industry. They're in something close to the structured bureaucracy type of thing.

I think the talk is there. We are family, over and over again. We are told we are family. You are told you are part of a family but you are dumped on every time you turn around. You don't trust anybody; you don't feel close to anybody. You keep being told that you're part of a family, but we are one major dysfunctional family. I think we are so dysfunctional. When I hear over and over what a family we are, to me a family means you care for me and you take care of me. [shouting] In my family, we took care of each other and we loved each other and we supported each other. We didn't dump on each other. We keep being told—it's lip service—we're being told because someone says that we should be a family. I think it's from the very top all the way down.

I think that probably the system says that you need to communicate, you need to show the staff that you care. And so, the chancellor puts out everything that shows that we are family and we care. Except he says it but nobody sees it; you don't feel it. There's no support. Everybody else has caught on. I don't think that I'm alone. The talk and the walk. It's almost kind of a joke now. Because the talk of the family is now the talk of the dysfunctional family. [laughs] Of course, a very good friend of mine says that in today's society the functional family is dysfunctional because if you're functional, you've got to be dysfunctional. And so, you throw it back and say, "Are we now so typical being dysfunctional that we're typical?"

We need to throw out the motivation being simply money and job security. If you are interested in teaching kids, the best teachers at the university are not the ones who have been promoted to the highest level or have gotten all of the accolades. They're the people who have always wanted to be good teachers and that's all they've cared about. Being dedicated. Regardless of whether or not he's— what is this idiot's name who has gotten the XYZ fellowship and is making $90,000 a year—never shows up for his classes, and when he does show up, he's ill-prepared. Never shows up for his guest lectures, but he publishes well and has convinced whatever that he's God's gift to whatever and there might be a handful of kids who think he's great but the rest think he's a joke. First he'd have to show up for class to teach, and he doesn't do that, so how could he be a good professor? But, by God, he's making $90,000 a year being the XYZ chair of the university. It is something that gives the university stature. It is something the university publishes all over, that they have this man who does all this. It makes us saleable. You know. Can you believe that we're expecting a group of Japanese business-people here to learn from him? Are we becoming too much of a business? Have they decided that's what sells the university? To have people like this.

MEANINGS AND LESSONS

Bonnie presents us with two themes. One is the con involved in referring to the university as a family (she's a marvelously penetrating critic). The second is her observation about the selling of the university. The con aspect is commonplace in industry and politics. The XYZ department chair story is her example of how dumb can magically become smart, again as in industry and politics.

LESSON

A university is like every other organization. They are compelled to play the game of social con to remain visible and competitive. By so doing, they pave the way for dumbness-rising-to-power.

She sees through the sham. What good does it do? She'll always do her job, reminding herself that while her employers may be weak she can be strong. She has empowered herself.

Bonnie's empowerment has a smart twist, coming without fanfare as a natural reaction to rewards ill-gotten and ill-gained.
She's saying, "You're the phony not doing your job. I'm doing
mine." The chancellor gives empowerment its dumb twist,
likening the university to a family. Bonnie, a clever cynic, says
it is a dysfunctional family.

THE VICE PRESIDENT AS ELEPHANT

This story is about how not to empower employees in a big-
time, prestigious corporation. The elevator whooshes us to
where division managers live, one floor under the vice presi-
dential suites. Here in this glass-skinned building bearing the
corporate name, we hear about frustration in muffled speech
in spite of the security of the setting. We enter an open area
with reception desks spotted at strategic points. A receptionist,
expecting us, says, "Hi, he'll be right back." Well-planned color
combinations lead the eye to modest offices with windows.
The man we have an appointment with is Chris, the division
human resources manager.

Chris is a 42-year-old bright, humorous, rapid talking,
quick-on-his feet manager with an MBA. He doesn't fit into or
like the authoritative, hierarchical style of his company. He
smiles easily, knows he has a good job, but is troubled by
inconsistencies and corporate self-deception. He owns a sub-
urban home and has two small children. His human resources
job is the interface between policy and people. Sometimes he
advises on personnel regulations, but primarily is involved in
executing policy for a division of thousands. He looks
harassed even though he says he's just returned from a brief
vacation. This is his elephant story. Names and places have
been changed.

> We were trying to get the union involved in a work redesign
> process. The presentation was to be made to them from our top man
> here, our VP of the business group. The idea was let's get the union
> on board and let's explain to them what the business case is and
> why we need to make some of the radical changes we need to
> make. Well, he delivers what is affectionately called the "burning

platform" case—why the business is changing on a global basis, all the economics you want to know. It's very factually based. I mean, these are engineers; they love facts. They deal with facts.

Now these are the union presidents from all the union locals all assembled in one meeting room. They show up, okay? You give this nice presentation for an hour or more.

A little lunch, you know, all that kind of stuff. And at the end, the appeal is built on, "Hey, we really want you but the train's leaving the station. If you're not with us, we're going for it anyway."

And I sat there and said, "Excuse me! Wait a minute now. How is that supposed to appeal to a group, that you're saying join us, especially when you have years of distrust that exists between the employees that are represented and management?" I mean just absolutely, absolutely classic.

That's the way it was billed. And the delivery, you know, is very factual so you know there is not a lot of appealing to emotion as much as it is, "Here are the facts. We gotta do this. Okay, you need some facts, obviously. You're not just going to do it to do it." You gotta, you know, show them there are some business reasons you want to do it. You want them as a business partner; present the case.

But I think about the closing at trying to invite people in and say, "Hey, Bill, you know I'm going forward. If you're with me, great. If not, train's leaving the station." You know, how does that appeal to you? It doesn't appeal to you very much.

If you don't join us, we're going to do what we feel we need to do. If you don't like it, you can't complain about it later. You can have input, but that doesn't mean veto power or anything. Management still has the prerogative to make the call. But this was an appeal to unions. You know, it became a real stiff-arm instead of, you know, embracing, the stiff-arm saying, "Well, you better join us, because if not, we're doing it without you."

Well, they know in the end they can't make the ultimate call. I think most employees recognize that management will make the call. It almost implies that you know what you want to do, so why are you asking me?

The union people? They asked us to walk out at that point, asked us to leave the room. I walked out of there, I knew, I said this was stupid. In fact, I went into the bathroom and a couple of my colleagues, guys from the field, were there and we said if only the boss had used a little more empathy today, we would have probably had a sale.

We went back into the room. A few of the guys had their jackets on, the baseball caps with the union logo, and all that on there. I said, "They're out of here." In fact, what I heard later was that several of them wanted to walk out. They stayed out of respect to the guy who keeps all of them together.

Their recourse? Well you sure know they could slow down. They were definitely angry. Afterwards, there were all sorts of wonderful pamphlets flying around from management. The union used it, self-serving for them. Put a slant on it, put fear into the members. You could predict the way they'd react based upon that kind of appeal.

I mean, you look at certain leaders and they are able to do it. Some of it's innate. You really can't learn that kind of thing. You know what I mean, in terms of charisma. The ability wasn't there; neither was the ability to internalize advice or counsel. I mean the emotional ability. I mean, if you look at the personality profile.

The system is reinforcing itself. I mean it continues to select the types of behavior that it wants. It's the way they do business. It's a blind spot. They're not doing anything wrong. But there's a cost to it. The time of all the people back at each site, sending messages back and forth, the loss of productivity because of the anxiety. You know, the common guy who's out there working on the shop floor, who is not even there at the meeting, he doesn't know what to believe. He doesn't know whether to believe union leadership or whether to believe management. He thinks, "I'm out of a job."

But the problem is they don't think they did anything wrong in the way they appealed that day.

MEANINGS AND LESSONS

Chris works on a floor below his boss in the corporate high-rise. Since their windows face the same direction, you would think they see the same scene. They don't. The late afternoon sun reminds Chris that he has work to bring home and he is churning. That same sun signals the beginning of a peaceful evening for his boss who is convinced he's been making the right decisions. When the two men nod to one another in the elevator, as they sometimes do, it's courtesy, not an acknowledgment of shared perceptions. Chris understands this. His boss, according to Chris, could care less. Chris reminds himself he was part of an important meeting and couldn't do anything.

Like cleanup crews that follow the elephants in circus parades, his job is to sweep things clean in the wake of the procession so that the street again looks normal. Elephants are majestic creatures, oblivious to what may be going on behind them.

LESSON

If they give you a broom and a scoop, it doesn't matter what title you have. You're real job is cleaning up after your leader.

Chris asks himself why he took this job. His vice president makes him uncomfortable. To make the job bearable, Chris feeds his boss information through memos, reprints, and books about enlightened management techniques—mentoring up—knowing he will seldom receive a reply. He's left hanging and wondering, as he felt during the meeting. As that meeting reached a crisis point, Chris was already starting to figure out damage control. It confirms his belief that his boss has lousy people skills. He once again becomes the firefighter.

LESSON

When you accommodate a dumb boss, you'll become something you won't like and may not even recognize.

But look again at this situation. Chris protects his integrity by fighting, complaining, and sometimes writing cynical memos. He gets away with it because his organization and many others know that the Chrises of the world will do their jobs well no matter how much they complain. Human resources people have professional codes of conduct and an identity beyond that defined by their employers. They work under fire and get comfort out of knowing that from time to time they make a true difference. Are they selling out? Chris is beginning to think he is, but most don't. They are energized by a common enemy, the leaders to whom they report who won't let them do the humane, decent things. Their running battles spice up their jobs.

LESSON

Human resources professionals blind themselves. That their leaders manipulate them is a certainty. That they manipulate their leaders is a delusion.

Chris had to move himself into his case-worker, smart-student role. "I know more than that guy," he thinks to himself. "That guy can act as if consequences don't matter, that I'll fix things for him. So what if it costs more?"

Chris knows that if he could reverse roles with his boss, conflicts would still exist. Chris's values condemn him to hard work—the doing of empathy and compassion for people. He will never understand his boss, although he thinks he understands him too well. What he does recognize, however, is that the system within which he works has been created by people like his boss. He, Chris, is the intruder and interloper. It is he, not his boss, who reads articles and books about the newest management ideas.

LESSON

The "fad of the week" is a program that management gives lip service to, but human resources people take seriously.

Chris's dream, and that of his colleagues within the company, is to be able to impart people skills to their powerful, autocratic leaders. The dream is a good one, but there is one thing that's been overlooked, and Chris (and all human resources people) should have recognized it a long time ago. The reason their management style hasn't changed much, the demon against which they continually fight, is in the following lesson.

LESSON

Leaders who deny their feelings seldom consider changing the way their organization treats its employees or customers.

WE GAVE HIM COMPLETE CONTROL

Family-owned restaurants are beautiful models for the study of empowerment gone wrong. They are self-contained societies. This story is about a privately owned restaurant with more than 100 employees. The woman telling us about intergenerational conflict is the second generation talking about the third. Cassie, known to everyone by her first name, could have had a career on the stage but instead performed daily on the one at the restaurant constructed by her mother where she starred for more than 25 years. She was the driver, the greeter, the charismatic center of everything that made customers feel good about being there.

She grew up in a family where her parents and grandparents were professors, lawyers, and businesspeople. She is a thin, wiry woman with a contagious laugh and a rollicking appreciation of life. Her mother, who used to tell her, "Grow where you're planted," started the restaurant, and Cassie grew up in it, married in it, and managed it with the help of her husband, a World War II veteran and business school graduate who loved working with his hands. They are retired, and their eldest son and his wife now run the business. There are strong disagreements about management style, handling personnel, and relationships with customers. The one item they do agree on is continuous expansion.

Cassie relates a major mistake her son made in hiring a floor manager, the position Cassie once filled. In the telling, we learn a good deal about the restaurant itself. Names and places have been changed.

When Lennie and I were considering retirement, we were staying longer and longer in West Palm. When you stay away from your business, you get less effective all the time, and even though we weren't retired, we were becoming less effective because other people were doing our work. I encouraged Mike (their son) to hire someone to step into my shoes.

Not knowing then that there was nobody to step into my shoes. It's hard on a family business. You can hire a manager, but it's still not like one of the family. And your customers are not going to accept any manager as one of the family.

So they (Mike and his wife, Judy) interviewed a number of people and hired this Paula. Well, it turns out that Paula had a lot of experience but did not have the love of the restaurant business or the knowledge to run an independent restaurant. She was a corporate person.

We had all this information coming in to us and we had our employees saying [screams the words], "You've got to get rid of this lady!" Mike hired her and I have to admit we weren't there. The headhunter recommended her and I nearly sued them because her whole résumé was a lie. They knew they were in trouble, but it wasn't worth it to us. Just get rid of her. Mike liked her and she did have a wonderful interview. She makes a wonderful first impression, but then our employees started calling us saying, "She's so terrible. She's undermining our enthusiasm. Everything that you built she's ruining."

She was doing her part [laughs] charging up fictitious customer complaints and pocketing the money. She was having "complaints" two or three times a night that never happened before. She was a thief. Then she'd pull things like, "I'm going to Albany to see my mother. Can I do anything for you?" Mike would say, "Sure, you can go and buy this secondhand restaurant piece." And we'd get the whole bill and Mike would say, "I guess I won't do that anymore." She'd send the manager home and have a party all night, give her friends all kinds of liquor. She had a sideline with the cleaning service.

She ended up killing herself, by the way. She shot herself. In the meantime, she stole our vacuum cleaner, too.

Mike is very reticent about confrontations and getting rid of people. He's afraid he'll get sued and stuff like that. He had an employment contract with her, and when she got there, she announced that she was suing the employer she just worked for. That was the clue. The headhunter and she were in cahoots on her résumé.

When the employees started to call, I called Mike and said, "Mike, what's this all about?" And he goes, "Well, she's, I think she'll be alright. But we're working with her, getting there." Stuff like that. Well it never happened. She didn't work out and I said, "I think you should get rid of her today."

The whole thing was stupid. He made a very serious error in judgment that affected our business. She was crazy. I would never have left her alone. I'd never hire her. Number one: The way she handled herself was inappropriate for a family business. You have to start at the bottom and find out what this family is all about. And you have to be humble enough to do every job in the restaurant. Find out what is making the place go and she wasn't willing to do that and I don't know that anyone would these days. Had Mike been right on her tail all the time, it might have turned out a little differently. My view of it is if I were hiring somebody to take my place, I would have worked with them for a year. I would never have left her alone, but independent restaurants are more trusting. I would not have hired her. She has got to be a workaholic, like myself.

She stayed so long because Mike hates confrontation and he always thinks it's going to get better. I like confrontation because it resolves things. That could be Lennie. Lennie hates confrontation, too. This was disastrous. I said, "Get rid of Paula!"

MEANINGS AND LESSONS

Both mother and son are the same in their own ways. The employees, who had to work with Paula, proved to be the smart ones. They saw a threat to their jobs, reported it, and in so doing told Mike, Judy, and Paula that they had no respect for them and, indeed, were not afraid of them. Cassie was present, even though she wasn't present. The employees were the ones being tumbled about in Paula's backwash, and they didn't like it.

===

LESSON

Employees are like canaries in a coal mine. When either chirp off-key, you know something's rotten in the environment.

===

Paula was hired to take Mike's mother's place, and in the process, the good mother was replaced by the bad mother.

Mike has trouble picking women. He never had to think about what to do with his mother around. Lennie, his father, couldn't help.

One way to understanding this episode is by looking into the past. Cassie was attractive to men and outshone her husband and children. No one in the family could compete with her. If, for example, someone called at home and got Lennie or Mike, they would automatically turn the call over to Cassie. But does the strong mother–weak son equation fully explain Mike's attraction to Paula? Is Cassie always the good mother? She wasn't when she permitted Mike to go unprepared into a key hiring process. She acknowledges that mistake. She wasn't when she allowed Paula to stay on the job for a year, knowing that it couldn't work. She knew that after 6 weeks, like her employees whom she trusted knew. Giving Mike more time under the guise of respecting his decision was even more hurtful because he had to live with pain.

LESSON

Forcing a manager to live with a mistake leads to chronic resentment and potential revenge.

For someone like Cassie, retirement means it's all over. What other activity could substitute for the pleasures of life on the stage? Try to see her as we did—fading and soon to be forgotten—no grand entrances, no applause, no curtain calls.

Cassie needs to get back in the scene, to find a life, tutor her son, and then leave the stage gracefully.

It isn't surprising to learn that many leaders of family businesses, especially those who have always been strong and dominant, do not leave gracefully. They hang on, as if hanging on will slow the hands of the clock. They fight, and some destroy what they've built in the process.

Castrating your offspring in a family business to appease the gods will not let you live forever.

YOU OWE ME

Try this charade: two professionals sitting across from one another not saying anything. Two lawyers, husband and wife, in a divorce proceeding? Wrong. Two psychoanalysts? Wrong. A chess match? Wrong. All the above are plausible. But let Roy tell you about it. We're in a restaurant in San Jose. Everyone seems to be driving a Beemer, a Jag, or a Mercedes. The noise masks our conversation. Names and places have been changed.

> I had a female manager, the only female manager I had, and she was a good person, one hell of an engineer, but as far as people management, she wasn't worth much. The reason was she gave you no direction. When you had one-on-ones with her, if you didn't talk, nobody talked. She didn't tell you what she wanted or expected from you. She didn't give you any goals to reach. She expected you to do all of it on your own. And I was just a supervisor. I was looking to my manager for direction and leadership. And I got none of it.
>
> The way she got that job was they had downsized and consolidated. We all thought they would give the job to my boss, who had been there for years. And then they wound up giving it to her. We were all flabbergasted. I never thought they'd give it to her. She had probably 100 people under her. I tell you this, I know that she's very much a feminist. She sent out 100 résumés when we were about to downsize and didn't get one reply. She was going to go so far as to change her name to a male name.
>
> Now she's a manager again of an even larger group. I don't believe that I could handle her position right now. Okay. I'm a manager, but if they offered me her job right now, I don't feel I could take it. Not because I don't have the capacity for doing it. But I guarantee you that if it was above her, she would take it just because she would feel they owed it to her.
>
> This lady was right out of the 1960s. She was prematurely gray

at 35. People would ask me, "Is that your mother?" She now dyes her hair and she's moved into the 1990s clothes styles only because she's in a position where she has to represent the company. Her boss actually came up to her and said, "You need to get some new clothes." I don't know if she's being promoted through the ranks because of who she knows and what she knows or if she's a woman and she knows enough. There are people who scratch their heads and say, "How did this person get here?"

But there are a lot of women who are promoted here because we need the quota. Absolutely. The federal government put the quota there, and in order for us to have federal contracts, we have to keep up with the quota. The same goes with race, color, creeds, and all that other stuff. The people who meet the quota may have some talent, but they weren't necessarily picked for their talent. They might carry the job so we could meet the quota.

MEANINGS AND LESSONS

Roy explains how quotas work in companies that get government contracts and how they worked in favor of a female engineer with no people skills. He isn't angry, just bewildered. She was his manager and a good engineer. He ridicules her "1960's femininity" although she was a baby during that decade. He picks on her hair color and choice of clothes—the ugly duckling lady engineer in a man's world. The consensus at his company was, "Huh? How did that happen?"

LESSON

Satisfying an affirmative action quota in order to obtain a federal contract takes priority over motivating employees and helping them learn.

A dumb female manager shouldn't be regarded as anything different from a dumb male manager. But society will do just that and look for special reasons to explain or excuse. Roy's confusion is caused by his manager's rapid progress. It happens to men. The most rapid progress is observed in powerhouse corporations ruled by supermacho men who elevate their offspring regardless of what. Women promoted above their intellectual or people-skills level are like society's offspring (in a special niche to be sure) helping big daddy get that contract. What's dumb about that?

EPILOGUE

The genesis of dumbness in the workplace starts back when one person was compelled to work for another and when working in groups became necessary for survival. Paleoanthropologists mark about 100,000 years ago as the time our ancestor hominid, *Homo erectus,* emerged into an early version of *Homo sapiens.* A form of human culture had to develop—at the earliest, perhaps 12,000 years ago according to experts—before dumbness in relationships became an element in social organization. Dumb acts undoubtedly took place among cave dwellers, but then as now, organized work was the defining experience.

From one person's ability to control another, we can segue to large-scale exercises of power. Taking slaves, wiping out enemies, extending territories, obtaining the favor of gods, creating priesthoods, and obeying rulers, emperors, and kings all confirm the paradigm of human dominance-submission. Work and power are unthinkable without discipline, control, and organization. And the highest expression of humanity's ability to organize has always been the military.

Dumbness, in the form we know it today, as a player in the unfolding of civilization, is only about 6000 years old. It makes its earliest appearance in print in Genesis. *Homo sapiens,* the big-brained hominid, had finally arrived.

Now for the stories told here. The most compelling observation is how people in power—from those who manage a small department to leaders of multinational corporations—believe they have the right to manipulate and play with the emotions of their employees. Granted, no one is a true slave, no one is tortured, and no heads are lopped off in these stories. There are no literal representations in our organizations of how people have been abused historically, although parts of the world (some in the United States still) carry on barbaric and inhumane practices. But only 60 years ago, millions in Europe were slaughtered by a "civilized" nation. And in the 1990s, there are genocidally inspired massacres. So our storyteller's lives are idyllic when measured against history and the abuses reported by Amnesty International. In one sense, these employees can be regarded as some of the luckiest people ever to walk the earth. So what's a little dumbness between friends?

Power, Technology, and Relationships

We'll tell you. The significance of dumbness in today's American workplace has to be understood in relation to what technological change has accomplished. From cries of greeting or warning, to drums, to lanterns swung in the night, to the signal semaphore, to telegraph, radio, telephone, and television, to the Internet, communication defines the form of organizations. The parallel in the evolution of the workplace is this: from slavery, to impressment, to long hours in unhealthy environments, to captive child and immigrant labor, to toxic physical conditions of employment, to plant shutdowns, to downsizing, to toxic emotional conditions, and to unhealthy relationships in the workplace. Dumbness is our name for the last two items on the list.

Communication and relationship modes are both on a continuum of how information is transmitted and how people interact with one another. The storytellers are describing incidents which leave people no less damaged in spirit and self-esteem than those told by early storytellers who spoke of natural and human-made catastrophes. What has to be grasped is today's sophisticated (Internet level) version of power exercised without regard to its emotional consequences. Consider the extent of depression in every level of society. Stress-induced disabilities are universally acknowledged. Burn-out is part of common parlance. The struggle to bring order to a chaotic worklife powers the sales of millions of self-help and lifestyle publications. We still bleed as our ancestors did, but internally and more slowly.

Fear and Compliance

What else do the stories say to us in addition to the role of power? Employees are compliant and fearful. Acceptance, resignation, tuning out, walking away, hoping to get the perpetrator's job, or moving on are survival techniques. None are growth-promoting ones, to be sure, but they are survival techniques nevertheless. Occasionally we hear about little games of getting even and of how to learn in a dumb environment. But how feeble. Even respondents who have some power cannot face up to the system. To jump back in time again, it's like all those thousands toiling for decades to build a pyramid in the desert.

Loyal to Dysfunction

Did you hear another refrain, a surprising one considering all that's been written about the death of loyalty? The negative construction of the phenomenon we want to discuss is that people become loyal to dysfunction. Your family is your family. As the people of Chicago used to say about the once-powerful congressman, Dan Rostenkowski (released from jail in August 1997), he may be a crook, but he's our crook. "Love my company" the first storyteller says.

There is a positive construction. People need to identify with images, icons, and organizations. Our school, our team, our city, our company baseball team, our company. If work is a good part of one's self-definition, then the boss though dumb and the organization though dysfunctional will retain a hold on people. We hear loyalty is latent, ready (eager may be too strong a word) to be evoked. Their actions reveal their thoughts—it can't be that bad or I wouldn't be here.

There Is Dysfunction

It is appropriate to use the concept of dysfunction to describe a workplace. Here we admit to taking a leap from a series of discrete episodes. It is a leap with which leaders will not agree. We rely, however, on many independent reports in addition to these stories.

Dysfunction means impairment. We received a phone call, "We have a dysfunctional board. They don't trust one another. Can you help us?" Dysfunction measured against what? How people could or should feel at work? How bosses should behave? How organizations should be run? Unless there is blatant criminal behavior or gross violations of laws and regulations promulgated for the public good and safety, do we have a right to tell someone how to run his or her business? Ordinarily not. Yet members of organizations feel something is wrong and must be changed.

Emotional distress, transient depressions, increased sick days, working at less than full potential, and working in a no-growth environment are unregulated behaviors. As yet they are not in the category of child labor laws, the 40-hour workweek, or OSHA regulations. The question is: Should they be? Is a dysfunctional workplace acceptable to society? Is a mean, stupid, and insensitive boss acceptable to society?

We don't think so, and saying that has nothing at all to do with bleeding-heart values. We're saying that reducing dumbness at the interpersonal level and within organizational cultures will make our corporations more globally competitive. That's what we all want, from Bill Clinton to Newt Gingrich to General Motors, IBM, Hewlett-Packard, Microsoft, and hundreds of new technology businesses.

Let's agree, for argument's sake, that what's just been pointed out is a desirable work plan. Smarter bosses and smarter organizations have competitive advantages. Change can't be accomplished overnight for the reasons already cited: love of power on one side and the passivity of survival in the face of overwhelming odds on the other. There is the smoking gun. We've shot ourselves in the foot by praying at the bottom-line altar. We've squelched the fire of enthusiasm out of our employees. Troy, tulipomania, Mississippi Scheme, Marshal Budënny, Vietnam, Valujet. We're right with you.

Dumbness is as dumbness does. "Hey, you don't want to bash my brains out with that bat, boss. Some day you might need me."

Lessons of Survival

We've called our storytellers some of the luckiest people in the world. They are surviving comfortably in physical terms but are paying an emotional price. If you were to ask, "Is it worth it?" we'd have to respond, "That's a nonquestion." They are, as millions of others like them, caught midstream in the turbulence of social change. As we watch them being carried along, what can we learn as they struggle to find calm waters and avoid organizational undertows? In other words, what *are* they doing to survive?

Pummelled by abusive power, demeaned, faced with double standards and confusing ground rules, unthanked, forced to swallow their pride, these storytellers (like all of us) are answering to a higher-order sanity. They are saving their companies by continuing to do their jobs as best as they know how. They are not dysfunctional even though their companies may be. They are smart in the best possible way by maintaining personal integrity working for companies that don't seem to care about integrity. They are the unacknowledged heroes of the technological revolution. They do what their bosses should be doing and learn from it. They care about their responsibilities. They work and perform in spite of the drain upon energy, self-esteem, and career ladders.

As we see them midstream, we learn that the American ethic of work, respect for work, and the doing because it has to be done are alive among citizen employees. As we hear them tell it, that same ethic does not exist (if it does, then minimally) among their bosses.

We learn they are surviving because they have no options. But what are they learning beyond survival? This: how to survive for longer periods and how to maneuver around the undertow. Those are necessary skills when you live day to day. Those are necessary skills when you're under siege. Imagine what these storytellers must be passing on to younger members of their occupations and professions. The legacy is that of a siege mentality, how to survive but not how to grow.

There are seldom final answers. A small insight that we have learned is: The ethics of smart employees need to be emulated by dumb bosses.

LESSON

Once power is in place, the true nature of an organization is revealed in how people do their jobs, not in people's perceptions of leaders.

REFERENCES

1. Burnam, T., *The Dictionary of Mis-Information,* 1975, Thomas Y. Crowell Company, New York.

2. Copper, C. L., and Payne, R., *Current Concerns in Occupational Stress,* 1980, John Wiley & Sons, New York.

3. Deming, W. E., *Out of the Crisis,* 1982, Massachusetts Institute of Technology, Cambridge, MA.

4. Duncan, M., and Weston-Smith, M. *Lying Truths,* 1979, Pergamon Press, Oxford.

5. Fussell, P., *Wartime: Understanding & Behavior in the Second World War,* 1989, Oxford University Press, New York.

6. Goldberg, M. H., *The Blunder Book,* 1984, William Morrow & Co., New York.

7. Goldhagen, D. J., *Hitler's Willing Executioners: Ordinary Germans and the Holocaust,* 1996, Alfred A. Knopf, New York.

8. Goleman, D., *Emotional Intelligence,* 1995, Bantam Books, New York.

9. Katzenbach, J. R., and Smith, D. K., *The Wisdom of Teams: Creating the High Performance Organization,* 1993, Harvard Business School Press, Boston, MA.

10. Katzenbach, J. R., *Real Change Leaders,* 1996, Harvard Business School Press, Boston, MA.

11. Kohut, J. J., and Sweet, R., *Dumb, Dumber, Dumbest: True News of the World's Least Competent People,* 1996, Penguin Books, New York.

12. Kowalski, R. M., Ed., *Aversive Interpersonal Behaviors,* 1997, Plenum, New York.

13. Lewin, K., *Field Theory in Social Science,* 1947, Harper, New York.

14. Loewen, J. W., *Lies My Teacher Told Me: Everything Your American History Textbook Got Wrong,* 1995, The New Press, New York.

15. Mackay, C., *Extraordinary Popular Delusions and the Madness of Crowds,* 1932, Farrar, Strauss & Giroux, New York.

16. Merry U., and Brown, G., *The Neurotic Behavior of Organizations,* 1987, Gestalt Institute Press, Cleveland, OH.

17. Noer, D. M., *Healing the Wounds,* 1993, Jossey-Bass Publishers, San Francisco, CA.

18. Ornstein, R., *The Evolution of Consciousness,* 1991, Prentice Hall, Englewood Cliffs, NJ.

19. Pelletier, K. R., *Healthy People in Unhealthy Places: Stress and Fitness at Work,* 1984, Delacorte Press, New York.

20. Peterson, D., and Hillkirk, J., *A Better Idea: Redefining the Way American Companies Work,* 1991, Houghton Mifflin, New York.

21. Regan, G., *The Book of Military Blunders,* 1991, ABC-CLIO, Santa Barbara, CA.

22. Rieber, R. W., *Manufacturing Social Distress: Psychopathy in Everyday Life,* 1996, Plenum, New York.

23. Shenkman, R., *Lies and Legends: Cherished Myths of American History,* 1988, William Morrow Co., New York.

24. Szasz, T., *The Myth of Psychotherapy,* 1978, Doubleday Anchor, Garden City, NY.

25. *The New York Times* Special Report, *The Downsizing of America,* 1996, Times Books, New York.

26. Tuchman, B. W., *The March of Folly,* 1984, Alfred A. Knopf, New York.

27. Van Fleet, J. K., *The 22 Biggest Mistakes Managers Make and How to Correct Them,* 1973, Parker Publishing, West Nyack, NY.

28. VandenBos, G. R., and Bulatao, E. Q., *Violence on the Job,* 1996, American Psychological Association, Washington, D. C.

29. Young, D., *Origins of the Sacred: The Ecstasies of Love and War,* 1992, Harper Perennial, New York.

INDEX

ABOUT THE AUTHORS

WILLIAM LUNDIN, Ph.D., and KATHLEEN LUNDIN are cofounders of
Worklife Productions, a consulting/training practice to every-
size corporation. They have trained managers and team leaders
for companies such as Ameritech, Hewlett Packard, Saturn,
Harley Davidson, Sun Microsystems, Johnson Hill Press, Jones
Dairy Farm, and M&M Mars, among others—and work on-site
or from Plowshares, their Frank Lloyd Wright-inspired Retreat
Center in the Kettle Moraine State Forest on Whitewater Lake,
Wisconsin. They are the authors of *The Healing Manager,*
*Building Positive Relationships at Work, Working with Difficult
People,* and *3 Values of Leadership.* They are widely recognized
for their straight-talking, interactive approach to workplace
problems grounded in solid therapeutic techniques. They can
be reached at N7411 Ridge Road, Whitewater, Wisconsin,
phone (608) 883-2229, fax (414) 473-7099.

With Illustrations by Steve Lundin.